PLAIN TALK ON Romans

Books by Dr. Gutzke . . .

Plain Talk About Christian Words
Plain Talk on Acts
Plain Talk on Luke
Plain Talk on Matthew
Plain Talk on John
Plain Talk on James
Plain Talk on Ephesians
Plain Talk on Exodus
Plain Talk on Genesis
Plain Talk on Mark
Plain Talk on Philippians
Plain Talk on Hebrews
Plain Talk on Romans
Plain Talk on Isaiah
Plain Talk on the Epistles of John
Plain Talk on Corinthians
Plain Talk on Galatians
Plain Talk on Timothy, Titus, and Philemon
Plain Talk on Peter and Jude
Plain Talk on Revelation
Plain Talk on Deuteronomy
Plain Talk on Thessalonians
Plain Talk on the Minor Prophets
Plain Talk on Leviticus and Numbers
Plain Talk on Colossians

PLAIN TALK ON Romans

MANFORD GEORGE GUTZKE
PH.D.

Lamplighter Books Grand Rapids, Michigan
Zondervan Publishing House

PLAIN TALK ON ROMANS

Lamplighter Books are published by Zondervan
Publishing House, 1415 Lake Drive, S.E.,
Grand Rapids, Michigan 49506

ISBN 0-310-25621-6

Library of Congress Cataloging in Publication Data

Gutzke, Manford George.
Plain talk on Romans.
1. Bible. N.T. Romans—Commentaries. I. Title.
BS2665.3.G87 227'.87'07 76-22516

Printed in the United States of America.

85 86 87 88 89 90 / 16 15 14 13 12 11

CONTENTS

PLAIN TALK ON Romans

Chapter 1

SALUTATION

(Romans 1:1-7)

Have you any idea why the apostle Paul wrote a letter to a group of persons who were already believers?

The Epistle to the Romans is a letter dealing with personal affairs, written by a preacher of the gospel of the Lord Jesus Christ to a group of Christians living in a city where he had never been. Why did he write it? Granted, the Christian message to mankind is "Be ye reconciled to God," but what would an apostle write about *after* many were reconciled? This is what we shall explore in this book.

Basically Paul wrote this letter to the Roman Christians to confirm their faith and to enable it to grow and expand. It is true that Christians are saved by faith, by believing. *Faith* is the noun; *believing* is the verb. But we know that believing requires that we have to have something to believe. And it would not be true to say we can be saved by believing just anything. It is like saying a man lives by swallowing. Of course there is a sense in which a man does live by swallowing; yet if a man would swallow poison, it would kill him. The swallowing itself would not be any different. Actually it is not the swallowing that counts: what counts is what one swallows. Just as it is the food we swallow that keeps us alive, so it is what and whom we believe that makes the difference in our spiritual lives.

It is common to say we are "saved by faith"; but what we actually mean is that we are saved by faith *in God through the Lord Jesus Christ.* So, if we want to improve, encourage, and strengthen this kind of believing, we need to know more and more what and whom we believe.

Paul had never been in Rome, and in writing to these people he knew nothing about their personal problems or experiences. He knew only that they were believers in Christ. What then would he write? I think he would tell them the same truth he would want all believers to have. When he heard there were a company of people in Rome who had started believing in Jesus, I feel he would immediately say, "I wish I could go there and tell them something." What would he tell them? This is what we will find in the Book of Romans.

The first seven verses of this epistle comprise the opening salutation or greeting. Here Paul explains what he understands about himself, about the Lord in whose name he writes, and about the believers to whom he is writing. Let us look at the words Paul uses: "Paul, a servant of Jesus Christ." This seems to be an ordinary statement. You know a servant to be someone who is doing something for somebody; but in the Greek the word used here brings out something more specific: "bondslave," a slave committed to his master forever. "Called to be an apostle." The word *called* refers to an assignment, like assigning a man to be the builder of your new house. You call on a doctor to treat your child, and you call on a mechanic to repair your car. Paul was called on to be an apostle; he was given the assignment to be responsible for the teaching that would be presented.

" . . . separated unto the gospel of God." This is a striking expression. Is it not true that when we think of separation we mean being separated *from?* But here it says "separated *unto.*" This is extremely important because when we speak of being separated we mean being taken out from among other men, being separated from, for some purpose. We are separated from because there is something we shall be separated unto. In the case of Paul, he was separated from everything natural, and during his earthly life in the course of God's leadership, he was "separated unto" the spiritual. He was to serve God. We observe that Paul lived a separated life. He understood his mission in the world was to be set apart for the purpose of teaching and preaching the good news of the salvation of God.

"Concerning his Son Jesus Christ our Lord, which was made of the seed of David according to the flesh." Jesus was born in Bethlehem of the tribe of Judah, of the house of David. He was made of the seed of David, and when He took human form He came to the family of David to be incarnate.

"And declared to be the Son of God with power, according to the spirit of holiness, by the resurrection from the dead." Paul, in looking at the Lord Jesus Christ, would say that the one thing which showed Him openly before the whole world to be the Son of God was His resurrection from the dead. Jesus had said this would be the only sign He would ever give of His work.

"By whom we have received grace and apostleship [Jesus was Paul's director, so to speak] . . . among whom are ye also called of Jesus Christ [Paul honored their call as believers as he did his own]: To all that be in Rome, beloved of God, called to be saints: Grace to you and peace from God our Father, and the Lord Jesus Christ."

We must keep these facts in mind from Paul's salutation: Paul was sent from God in the name of the Lord Jesus Christ. He was writing to these people who believed in Jesus that he might tell them more about the gospel, and what God would do for them in Christ Jesus.

Chapter 2

PAUL'S ATTITUDE TOWARD OTHER BELIEVERS

(Romans 1:8-12)

Have you ever considered why a great preacher would be grateful for other believers?

"First, I thank my God through Jesus Christ for you all." This is how the apostle Paul wrote about the Christians who lived in Rome. He had never met these people personally but he had heard of them, and here he reveals his feelings.

The essence of spiritual living is based on believing. What do we mean by this? Believing is our confidence that what God has promised He is able to perform. This kind of believing is not make-believe; it is being totally convinced that a certain promise will come to pass. It is not always easy; such confidence needs the support of other believers.

A person who accepts Christ believes in God, who is invisible, and believes about what God will do. But when a person deals with matters in this world so that they press in on him, things that are invisible and eternal become dim. Soon this person begins to wonder whether his spiritual beliefs are really true. To have one's faith remain strong it is essential that faith be fed and nurtured. Many are troubled from time to time because their faith is weak. If a person becomes conscious of the fact that his faith is weak, he should thank God that he is now aware of it. He knows what to do: feed it. It is always an encouragement for a Christian to be associated with others who believe in Christ. If someone has questions in his mind about his faith, it is important that he seek out other persons who believe and associate with them. Look closely at verse 8: "I thank my God through Jesus Christ for you all, that your faith is spoken of throughout the whole world." The faith of those Roman believers was talked about and that was encouraging to

Paul. In Acts 28:15 there is cited an incident when Paul was being taken as a prisoner to Rome. Certain believers met him on the road "whom when Paul saw, he thanked God, and took courage." Here is the importance of public testimony. Believers are a city set on a hill for all to see. We should let our light shine, "that men might see [our] good works and glorify [our] Father which is in heaven" (Matt. 5:16). It is not good to hide our light under a bushel.

> For God is my witness, whom I serve with my spirit in the gospel of his Son, that without ceasing I make mention of you always in my prayers; making request, if by any means now at length I might have a prosperous journey by the will of God to come unto you (Rom. 1:9,10).

The fact that Paul prayed for his fellow believers again and again, thanking God for their faith, cannot be stressed too strongly. Is it clear to others around you that you really are a believer? Now note the humble prayer Paul offers, "Making request [not demands], if by any means now at length I might have a prosperous journey." He had looked forward to this for a long time and he thinks perhaps now the time has come. ". . . I might [he isn't saying he is sure] have a prosperous journey by the will of God to come unto you."

In planning to visit Rome, Paul put his quest before God, then waited on God. Are you praying about something special? Note Paul's prayer; fix its pattern in your mind. Be careful that you pray "if it be *Thy* will, not mine." Paul had a practical reason for his prayer: he wanted to visit the Christians in Rome, and he hoped it would be in the will of God for him to do so.

> For I long to see you, that I may impart unto you some spiritual gift, to the end ye may be established (Rom. 1:11).

What was the spiritual gift Paul wanted to share with them? Certainly it was not money nor empowering them to do something. Perhaps it was a gift of insight. Paul had seen something in the gospel: he had seen the truth. He had come to an understanding about living in the Lord, and he felt it could be helpful to them.

I think the best illustration of the word *established* is the following: Have you ever transplanted anything? The problem is whether or not the new plant will grow. You are interested in whether it will become "established," which would occur if new roots thrust forth. You believe in Jesus Christ — now find out what this means in your business, to your family and friends, and in other areas of your life. As you recognize what your faith means in each facet of your experience, you will find your faith holding up under all these circumstances. It is this realization that will establish you. This can be achieved through experience, study, and understanding; and it will enable you to grow stronger.

> For I long to see you, that I may impart unto you some spiritual gift, to the end ye may be established; that is, that I may be comforted together with you by the mutual faith both of you and me (Rom. 1:11,12).

Chapter 3

NOT ASHAMED OF THE GOSPEL

(Romans 1:13-17)

Do you understand why Paul was so confident when he preached the gospel?

> For I am not ashamed of the gospel of Christ: for it is the power of God unto salvation to every one that believeth (Rom. 1:16).

In this portion we see that Paul goes on record about his personal confidence in the gospel he preached; in a sense he shows his own attitude toward the gospel. I suspect we may be inclined to think that a man like Paul would be bold because he was a bold man or to think he was strong in faith because he was an energetic character. But this is not the case. Paul was bold because he was absolutely certain the gospel would work. He was confident not because he was brash in disposition, but he was convinced of the power of the gospel.

> Now I would not have you ignorant, brethren, that oftentimes I purposed to come unto you, (but was let hitherto,) that I might have some fruit among you also, even as among other Gentiles (Rom. 1:13).

The old English word *let* actually means "was hindered." If you have played tennis you will remember when a certain play is made and a certain event happens, we say that the ball was "let." Just as a tennis ball hits the top of the net and being so hindered is a "let" ball, so a person can be hindered. Paul had been hindered in his plans to visit Rome.

In verse 14 the apostle says, "I am debtor both to the Greeks, and to the Barbarians." In verse 15 he says, ". . . I am ready to preach the gospel to you." And in verse 16 he claims, "For I am not ashamed of the gospel of Christ. . . ." We can put these three statements together to see how Paul felt about himself:

In verse 14: "I am debtor."
In verse 15: "I am ready."
In verse 16: "I am not ashamed."

"I am debtor" means "I feel under obligation to get this done"; "I am ready" means "I am ready to go right now; I have no hesitation whatever"; "I am not ashamed" means "I have every confidence in the outcome." Paul speaks of being debtor both to the Greeks and to the "Barbarians." (Barbarians were not rough, crude people. It was customary for the Greeks to refer to anyone who was not Greek as a "barbarian.") Sometimes one considers himself a debtor because he has received something from someone else. Paul had been given a message to deliver *to* these people. He had not received anything *from* them, but he had received something *for* them. He was a messenger who had been entrusted with a package to be delivered to a certain address, and he was responsible for it; he was obligated to deliver it.

Paul had been given the gospel to take to all men, both to the Greeks (the educated people) and to the Barbarians (the uneducated people). "So, as much as in me is, I am ready to preach the gospel to you that are at Rome also." He was ready to preach the gospel anywhere, at any time, because it was always relevant. "I am not ashamed of the gospel of Christ. . . ." This was not because Paul was a shameless character, but because he had every confidence in the gospel: ". . . for it is the power of God unto salvation to every one that believeth; to the Jew first, and also to the Greek." Naturally he would go to the Jew first, because the Jew understood so much of the gospel already. But he would also go to the Greek who did not have that heritage. "For therein is the righteousness of God revealed from faith to faith." In the preaching of the gospel the righteousness of God is revealed as being realized through faith.

Chapter 4

WITHOUT EXCUSE

(Romans 1:18-20)

Do you realize that anyone can perceive truth about God? There is no excuse for anyone not to recognize Him.

> Because that which may be known of God is manifest in them; for God hath showed it unto them (Rom. 1:19).

The apostle Paul seems to be declaring this truth in his Epistle to the Romans. As we read these verses we find Paul's blunt affirmation that the truth of God is so obvious any person can know it. Paul points out that for anyone to say he cannot believe there is a God, is for a man to admit he is a fool. The psalmist had written the same long before: "The fool hath said in his heart, There is no God" (Ps. 14:1). The apostle picks up this idea and discusses mankind in general, noting mankind's attitude and relationship to God. Here Paul claims that the reality of God is so clearly set forth in nature that anyone can recognize there is a God.

It is common for man to claim there is no real evidence of God. Paul challenges this. He says plainly that everyone has evidence of God, and God holds them responsible for it.

> For the wrath of God is revealed from heaven against all ungodliness and unrighteousness of men, who hold the truth in unrighteousness; because that which may be known of God is manifest in them; for God hath showed it unto them (Rom. 1:18,19).

All the actions of men bring results: "Whatsoever a man soweth, that shall he also reap" (Gal. 6:7). Any action that transgresses the law of God, that breaks the Ten Commandments, is sin. Such actions are motivated by the selfish desires of man, who wants things for himself that are contrary to the nature of God. Man is responsible for his desires. Paul states that right actions are so obviously right the only way they can be obscured is by willful sin.

God ensures in the natural processes that certain things follow certain things; this is obvious. For example, observe creation. Whether you look at the earth or the sky, trees or animals, you know there must be a Creator. When you see a machine, you know there is a mechanic. If you see a picture, you know there is an artist. The freedom you have to turn to the right or to the left makes you responsible for whichever way you choose to go. These are fundamental realities. Paul says enough is known by such things to guide a man in right ways. If a person goes wrong, it is his own fault; he is without excuse.

Acting in ungodliness and in unrighteousness obscures and buries the truth of God. This is the meaning of "who hold the truth in unrighteousness" (v. 18). The English translation is not as good as it could be, because the Greek verb means more than the word *hold.* A good translation would be "hold down the truth in unrighteousness." The truth of "holding down" can be seen in what happens to grapevines. Wherever they are cultivated men build racks or arbors to guide their growth, frames to lift them off the ground so they will produce grapes. If the plant lies on the ground, it will not produce grapes. That is what the apostle Paul is saying.

This truth — recognizing the reality of God — is within everyone. My own sinful conduct, being proud and self-indulgent, is like gathering trash and putting it on top of the grapevines. They will not produce grapes. When I do only what *I* want to do I am obscuring the truth of the reality of God.

> For the invisible things of him from the creation of the world are clearly seen, being understood by the things that are made, even his eternal power and Godhead; so that they are without excuse (Rom. 1:20).

The heavens declare the glory of God; the firmament shows His handiwork (Ps. 19:1). The whole created world reveals the nature of God. The Apostles' Creed begins, "I believe in God the Father Almighty, Maker of Heaven and earth." God made all things. No one can escape this blunt indictment of his attitude toward God. Each person should know enough about God to be careful of his conduct and to know that he will answer for what he does. He knows he should not offend or take advantage of other people; he should not steal or lie. If he goes on the wrong path it is because he chooses to. This is what the apostle Paul is saying: if anyone acts in a way that is contrary to the will of God — unholy, ungodly, and unrighteous — the wrath of God is revealed against him. That person is without excuse.

Chapter 5

TURNING AWAY FROM GOD

(Romans 1:21-32)

How does a person become a fool?

> Because that, when they knew God, they glorified him not as God, neither were thankful; but became vain in their imaginations, and their foolish heart was darkened. Professing themselves to be wise, they became fools (Rom. 1:21,22).

In this first chapter of Romans Paul begins by examining the condition of men. It is as if he were going to answer the questions, Why do men need to be saved? What is their condition that they need to be saved? At the outset Paul points out that man has foolishly turned away from God. In verses 21-32 we see that he is emphasizing again that there is plain evidence in nature of the reality of God, and man has been a fool to ignore the evidence that God exists.

There are a number of steps by which man turns away from God. This passage describes the classic pattern, because this has always been the way a man turns away from God: "Because that, when they knew God, they glorified him not as God." They knew there was a God but they did not act toward Him as if He were God. ". . . neither were thankful." If a person fails to recognize who God is and that He created everything, he will also fail to thank Him. If a man neglects to give thanks to God, he is opening the door for all manner of evil in his soul. Then this follows immediately: ". . . but became vain in their imaginations."

Why would these people become vain, proud in their imaginations? Because they praised themselves. Because of this "their foolish heart was darkened." Whenever we see the word *fool* in the Bible we can always bear in mind "The fool hath said in his heart, There is no God." A foolish heart does not recognize God, nor does it possess wisdom. "Professing themselves to be wise, they became fools." This is always the direction a foolish person goes, taking the positive position that he knows something. These people were acting as if there were no God, then they took the position there is no God. When they became fools, notice what happened: ". . . and changed the glory of the uncorruptible God into an image made like to corruptible man, and to birds, and four-footed beasts, and creeping things."

Men had to have some view of God; after all, the name of God is in the mind of man. But when they stopped giving Him honor, they began to make something else out of Him, treating Him as if He were only a man, and this impaired their concept of God. Step by step they proceeded into the dark until they finally changed their idea of God. Next follows a detailed account of how God handled them, as seen in verses 24, 26, and 28: "Wherefore God also gave them up to uncleanness" (v. 24); verses 24 and 25 tell why and how. "For this cause God gave them up unto vile affections" (v. 26). He actually allowed them to become infected with ugly things. In verse 28 we have the climax: "And even as they did not like to retain God in their knowledge, God gave them over to a reprobate mind."

Men did not want to think about God so He let them go, and then they could not think about anything correctly. There is a progression away from God; a person does not turn away all at once. He goes step by step; one thing leads to another. There is a growth in unbelief. It may start with some knowledge of God, but when the person does not honor Him as God, soon he does not recognize Him as God. He raises questions about Him which, of course, means he is not thankful for what he has. When this happens all these other things follow. The person becomes vain in his imaginations; the foolish heart is darkened; "professing themselves to be wise, they became fools, and changed the glory of the uncorruptible God into an image made like to corruptible man. . . . Wherefore God also gave them up to uncleanness through the lusts of their own hearts. . . . And even as they did not like to retain God in their knowledge, God gave them over to a reprobate mind."

So reads the sad story of men who have turned away from God.

Chapter 6

CRITICS WILL BE CONDEMNED

(Romans 2:1-11)

Do you realize that when one criticizes other people it actually makes a difference in the critic's standing before God?

> Therefore thou art inexcusable, O man, whosoever thou art that judgest (Rom. 2:1).

Paul is showing that all men face the judgment of God. In the Book of Romans he opens up the meaning of the gospel to help believers understand more of what the gospel promises are. He also describes the condition of man. In the first chapter Paul pointed out that a man should be thankful for everything and that neglecting thanksgiving fosters in man vain and foolish ideas.

In the second chapter Paul draws attention to other factors that cause persons to be responsible before God. As the chapter opens he states that the human capacity to criticize, to judge the actions of others, shows a person's responsibility to judge himself. Because man has the capacity to judge, he is responsible for his own conduct. This does not mean that criticizing other people brings on our own judgment, but it shows that our capacity to judge others is what makes us liable to judgment. Our own guilt is grounded in what each of us actually does wrong.

Paul points out that God's judgment of conduct is realistic and factual. "The judgment of God is according to truth against them which commit such things" (Rom. 2:2). God is affected not only by what we do in the way of criticizing, He judges by the way we act in ourselves. In the third verse Paul is anxious that we should be aware of coming judgment and feel our guilt:

> And thinkest thou this, O man, that judgest them which do such things, and doest the same, that thou shalt escape the judgment of God? (Rom. 2:3).

If we are able to see the faults in other people, do we think God will not see the faults in us? We are often tempted to think that because we see faults in other people and condemn them, that somehow we are considered all right. It is somewhat like three men who have been involved in a crime; one of them turns state's evidence and blames the other two, and he is then allowed to go free. That would not make any difference to God, who already knows who is responsible. He who turns state's evidence is only indicating all the more that he knew it was wrong, and such a person certainly will not be entitled to immunity.

> To them who by patient continuance in well doing seek for glory and honour and immortality, eternal life: But unto them that are contentious, and do not obey the truth, but obey unrighteousness, indignation and wrath, tribulation and anguish, upon every soul of man that doeth evil, of the Jew first, and also of the Gentile (Rom. 2:7-9).

The way this is written could give some people the impression that it is our works that make the difference. It is true that what we do matters, but here we must watch our language. Remember that one thing we do is either believe in the Lord Jesus Christ or not believe in Him. Our outward performance is seen by God, but we must remember that He also sees our inward performance. Welldoing includes the idea of continuing to believe in the Lord. In John 6:28,29, when the people asked Jesus what they should do that they might work the works of God, He said, "This is the work of God, that ye believe on him whom he hath sent." If we, therefore, are patiently continuing in welldoing, one of the things we are doing well is believing in the Lord Jesus Christ.

At the same time, this is an important corrective about faith. Faith is not just a matter of something in the mind; it comes out in the actual performance. To "them that are contentious, and do not obey the truth," this is unbelief. They are contentious about the revelation from God, and they do not obey the truth about the revelation of God — this is unbelief. We will note the reward: "eternal life, glory, honour, and peace, to every man that worketh good." But we must also note the punishment: to them that do not obey the truth, "indignation and wrath, tribulation and anguish, . . . of the Jew first and also of the Gentile." This is true for the person who never heard of religious matters. The judgment of God is fair but it is sure.

Chapter 7

CONSCIENCE WILL BE THE JUDGE

(Romans 2:12-16)

Do you recognize that conscience in our living and acting is as natural to man as the sense of balance in walking?

No doubt many of us give little thought to our capacity of conscience. We may know quite well what it is to have the feeling something is wrong or that such and such is what we should do, but we may not realize this is a faculty given to us in our creation. We are made this way. It is a matter of being equipped with a sort of built-in evaluator, as if each of us had a sort of gyroscope within to keep us on an even keel. Perhaps you have seen a toy built on that principle, so that if the wheel turns fast enough the device will stay at whatever angle it is put. Conscience works as a stabilizer so that we are not easily confused about our values. Conscience is a faculty given to each of us to help keep us straight.

If you have a feeling that you are leaning over and that you want to straighten up, the principle that keeps you walking upright is your inward feeling of balance. Even if you shut your eyes when you lean over, you will know you are leaning. This is the way your conscience works: it in inherent in each person. It does the same thing that the Ten Commandments do.

The Ten Commandments were given to men for their help, to show what is right and wrong. They function much like the white fences along the roads in the mountains. A person driving along a mountain road, which winds around the hillsides so that he has only a limited space to drive safely, finds it helpful to have a row of white fence posts to mark the safety limit for driving. When the driver stays on his side of those white posts, he will be safe. The fence posts themselves cannot keep the driver on the road — he can ignore them — but they can help him a great deal by showing him where safety lies. It is the same with the law. The law cannot keep a soul on the right road, but it is intended to be a real help in showing precisely where the road is: what is right and what is wrong.

This is how the Ten Commandments operate, and this is how conscience operates. Such a function of conscience, the feeling of what is right or wrong, exists within everyone. Babies show its operation. Long before they are old enough to talk they know whether they are doing what their parents want them to do. It is readily seen how they will do something and then look quickly to see if the parents noticed. Man's conscience is not the result of instruction or training. Of course, instruction sharpens the sense of what is right and wrong, and training makes a person sensitive to this feeling and alert to it; but the faculty is there originally, just like the faculty of vision. A person can improve his eyesight and make it sharper by training and exercise; but eyesight is a faculty he is born with, a faculty that can be improved or impaired.

Conscience can also be improved. A person can become more and more sensitive to what is most right and wrong by noting actual facts and consequences and by becoming more alert to it. On the other hand, one may digress to the point where his conscience will not bother him at all. If a person never pays attention to his conscience, it will grow weaker, like any other faculty.

However, if a person is sensitive to his conscience and willing to stop what he is doing while he checks things over, he will find that his conscience will quickly show him whether he was acting wisely or not. Conscience is like a property line. Outside big buildings downtown there are brass plates embedded in the sidewalks with the words *Property Line* on them. These indicate the limits of the land that belongs to the company. If the property-line marker were not there, that land could be lost to the public street. That property-line marker does not keep a person from stepping over it, but it does show where the property ends.

As it is with the law, so it is with the conscience. When one ignores his inner feelings and knowingly continues to do wrong, he is guilty in the sight of God. Even if he did not have that feeling he would be judged, but not in exactly the same way. He would not be as guilty as when he acts contrary to what he knows is right.

In one sense, conscience is like a thermometer. There are naive people who believe that having a thermometer makes the days hotter or the nights colder, as the case might be. I knew farmers in Canada who did not want to have a thermometer because with one the days seemed colder. But the thermometer merely records the temperature. Conscience is like that: it simply shows whether something is right or wrong. Some people think that because they *know* what is right, they are free; but it is what they actually *do* that counts.

Paul argues that anyone who has a conscience and does wrong is guilty. Until now he has mentioned three different ways in which sin can be seen. In the first chapter he pointed out that men are guilty because of the light of nature. They could know from nature that they should be thankful for what they have. If they are not thankful and become vain, ignoring God, they are guilty. In the early part of the second chapter it was revealed that if any person has the capacity to judge other people, he is guilty, because if he is able to criticize others he is able to criticize himself. Not only has he done wrong, but he knew it was wrong when he did it.

Finally there is the matter of conscience, which is another evidence of sin. It is the general idea that a person actually has an awareness of what is right and wrong, yet many times does the very thing he feels is wrong, which makes his sin doubly offensive to God. Paul is anxious to point out that there is not as much to show how to be right, as to show what is wrong; thus men need a Savior, and they have Him in Christ Jesus.

Chapter 8

OUTWARD PROFESSION WILL NOT HELP

(Romans 2:17-24)

Do you understand that being acquainted with and taking part in religious practices is no assurance that you are personally right with God?

> Thou therefore which teachest another, teachest thou not thyself? (Rom. 2:21).

Paul now pays special attention to the Jew: "Behold, thou art called a Jew, and restest in the law, and makest thy boast of God" (v. 17). The word *Jew* does not refer only to the blood descendants of Abraham. A man could become a Jew if he accepted the teachings and the culture of the Jews. When we speak of a Jew, we refer to a person who has been trained in a certain way. It will be helpful to keep in mind that Paul is not limiting his words to the Jewish nation, but he is speaking to every person who has been brought up to know the promises of God to Abraham and to David (i.e., for any person who has been instructed in the Scriptures). This would include the children of Christian parents. The Jew has confidence in the Scriptures. He makes his boast of God because he feels sure God is on his side. This person has been instructed in the Scriptures. To this person Paul asks the question, "Thou therefore which teachest another, teachest thou not thyself?"

Paul is aware that those who have been brought up this way might be snared into thinking they are better than others. It is easy to think that because we know what is in the Bible we may be better than other people. While it is a benefit for us to know these things, it does not make us any better. When we teach others what is right and wrong, we may be inclined to think that we are better than they. But actually, as Paul points out, our knowledge only makes us that much more responsible for how we act. There are many advantages we who have been brought up among Christian people have. Some of these have already been mentioned. ". . . restest in the law." It is surprising how many people feel they have security because they know what is in the Bible; they are almost inclined to think it belongs to them. ". . . and approvest the things that are more excellent." It is wonderful to be brought up in a good home and a good church and community; such a person knows right from wrong better than others. ". . . which hast the form of knowledge and of the truth in the law" (Rom. 2:17-20).

Here Paul is saying that the actual outline of Scripture is the outline of the truth, the outline of the knowledge of God. But it is not a matter of just knowing the law — we must obey its commands. Notice this expression, "through breaking the law dishonourest thou God?" Is it possible that when we know what the Bible teaches and then ignore those teachings, we really are dishonoring God? Many in the church teach things the Bible does not discuss; they would be shocked to learn that they are thus dishonoring God.

It will be helpful to think of the word *Jew* as representing those who have grown up in religious homes and have done church work, and who are thus more responsible to walk in the ways of God.

Chapter 9

ONLY GENUINE OBEDIENCE COUNTS

(Romans 2:25-29)

Do you know that it is your intentions behind your religious acts that count?

"For he is not a Jew, which is one outwardly." To help us understand this, Paul uses the example of circumcision, one of the Jewish ceremonies. Here is important truth to remember, especially when we celebrate the sacraments: The outward action is meaningless unless while performing it we have in mind its true meaning. Let me remind you that Paul speaks about the Jew as someone who has been trained in religious matters. Paul uses circumcision as an illustration of a rite that is practiced to express a belief. We can think of circumcision as a type of baptism, for instance, or as a type of the Lord's Supper.

Paul writes, "For circumcision verily profiteth, if thou keep the law." I suppose everyone knows that circumcision was a ceremony that was practiced by the Jews upon infant boys. The mark of this surgical operation was evidence that the infant had been circumcised and was now considered to be in the covenant of Abraham, because this was done in the tradition of his faith. And if the parents followed in obedience the way Abraham walked, the circumcision was meaningful. ". . . but if thou be a breaker of the law, thy circumcision is made uncircumcision."

There are various ways we can understand this. The significance of a wedding ring is that the circular band implies an unending love on the part of an individual. A person could be married who does not wear a wedding ring, but it is a valid sign of marriage if the one wearing it is sincere about it. It could be true, but it cannot do anything for the person, and this is what Paul implies about the ceremony of circumcision.

> Therefore if the uncircumcision keep the righteousness of the law, shall not his uncircumcision be counted for circumcision? And shall not uncircumcision which is by nature, if it fulfil the law, judge thee, who by the letter and circumcision dost transgress the law? (Rom. 2:26,27).

In other words, if the people who have not been circumcised follow through in obedience as the Word of God requires, it will be counted just as if they had been circumcised. And if those who have been circumcised disobey God, won't those who follow the Word of God judge them?

> For he is not a Jew, which is one outwardly; neither is that circumcision, which is outward in the flesh (Rom. 2:28).

This is the gist of the passage. A person cannot be considered a Jew simply because he says he is one or because of what has been performed outwardly in the flesh, "but he is a Jew, which is one inwardly." One must be sincere in his belief to truly be a Jew.

> And circumcision is that of the heart, in the spirit, and not in the letter; whose praise is not of men, but of God (Rom. 2:29).

Baptism is of the heart, in the spirit, and not in the outward performance. This individual's praise comes not from men but from God. Such a person may be counted a believer.

Chapter 10

THE ADVANTAGE OF RELIGIOUS TRAINING

(Romans 3:1-19)

Are you aware that while religious training and public practices are not able to save you, such things are nevertheless important?

> What advantage then hath the Jew? or what profit is there of circumcision? (Rom. 3:1).

While formal religious practices are inadequate to save the soul they are not altogether useless. Paul discusses this. About the value of formal services he says,

> Much every way: chiefly, because that unto them were committed the oracles of God (Rom. 3:2).

The Jews were instructed in the Bible. Today we would have to say this about church members because they are instructed in the Bible. It was beneficial to be a Jew, mainly because the Scriptures were given to the Jewish people; and by the same token it is a great benefit to go through church practices, which are outward religious exercises, since those practices often set forth the Scriptures.

> For what if some did not believe? shall their unbelief make the faith of God without effect? (Rom. 3:3).

Suppose some of the people who go through these exercises are not sincere. Does that mean the other people who are sincere will not get anything out of it? Not at all. In the spring fruit trees are covered with blossoms. Yet not every blossom produces fruit, because many blossoms fall to the ground. If we had no blossoms there would be no fruit. With regard to your church life, although some prayers may be offered in a perfunctory manner, they all point to God. This does have an effect. If you attend a church where worshipers read their prayers, it may sound as if they are moving along together in lock step. One might have the impression they do not mean what they are saying, but in this ritual the printed words themselves are good.

Paul would claim that while many may not be sincere when reading their ritual prayers, there would still be some truth in the exercise: "Let God be true, but every man a liar" (Rom. 3:4). Even if the people do not mean what they are saying, the words are still true. Thus, while the Communion service in some churches may seem to be routine, it does present the truth.

In Romans 3:10-18 Paul emphasized his point that "there is none righteous, no, not one . . . There is none that seeketh after God. They are all gone out of the way . . . there is none that doeth good, no, not one. . . . There is no fear of God before their eyes." Paul concludes by saying, "Now we know that what things soever the law saith, it saith to them who are under the law: that every mouth may be stopped, and all the world may become guilty before God" (Rom. 3:19).

Paul has been emphasizing that everyone needs the salvation of God in Jesus Christ. He has a gospel of which he is not ashamed, a gospel that can save to the uttermost those who come to God through the Lord Jesus Christ.

Chapter 11

RIGHTEOUSNESS BY FAITH

(Romans 3:20-26)

Do you realize that Jesus Christ provides in the gospel all that you need to stand in the presence of God as if you had never done wrong?

> Being justified freely by his grace through the redemption that is in Christ Jesus (Rom. 3:24).

These are the words used by the apostle Paul as he sets forth the amazing truth that a person may be made right in the sight of God through Christ Jesus by the grace of God. This particular portion of Romans is difficult to understand unless one studies it carefully. Paul is showing the deeper meaning of the work of Jesus Christ on our behalf that salvation may be available to everyone who believes.

> Therefore by the deeds of the law there shall no flesh be justified in his sight: for by the law is the knowledge of sin (Rom. 3:20).

The expression "deeds of the law" refers to our conduct wherein we try to keep rules and regulations, doing what we should do, and thereby trying to qualify for the blessing of God. Someone might ask, "Isn't that all right?" It would be all right if it were possible. "Wouldn't it be all right for you to want to swim if you were in danger of drowning? Wouldn't you want to swim as far as you could?" Yes, but if you were 200 miles from shore the swimming wouldn't make much difference.

Paul has pointed out that our guilt is such that we could not make things right even if we wanted to. He adds that the law was given so we would know right from wrong, yet this in itself does not enable us to do right. It is unreasonable to use the law to try to make a man right before God. A thermometer will tell us how hot or cold it is, but it will not give any heat. A tape measure will not sew a dress; it is solely for measuring. The law tells us what is right and wrong, but it does not make us do right.

> But now the righteousness of God without the law is manifested (Rom. 3:21).

There is a way to be right with God, apart from keeping a set of rules. In the Bible "right" means being straight up and down. It is natural for us as human beings to want to work at becoming like this; but what Paul is talking about is the righteousness which comes from God, that is, being right because God does it in us. This is the new covenant, and we shall be referring to it from time to time.

> Even the righteousness of God which is by faith of Jesus Christ unto all and upon all them that believe: for there is no difference (Rom. 3:22).

This righteousness, which is produced by God in us, comes by faith; it comes from Jesus Christ when we believe in Him. Being right with God is a matter of our attitudes and the values we cherish, a matter of the goals for which we strive. It cannot be achieved in our own strength. It will appear in us by the Holy Spirit, who will write the law of God on our hearts; leading us in the will of the Lord Jesus Christ to do the will of the Father. The necessary condition is that we believe in Christ, that we commit ourselves to Him as our Savior and Lord. This is true both for the Jew and Gentile.

Two men are in a lifeboat: one can swim; the other cannot. But they are equally safe, and both will get to shore. What gets both men to shore is the lifeboat. Earlier Paul argued that the Jew has an advantage: it is advantageous to have had religious training in the home, but that is not enough. Each person needs Jesus Christ.

> Being justified freely by his grace through the redemption that is in Christ Jesus (Rom. 3:24).

This work of grace, being made just, is free, without obligation. The "redempton that is in Christ Jesus" is the opportunity to be redeemed that is offered in and through Jesus Christ. "Whom God hath set forth to be a propitiation through faith in his blood" (Rom. 3:25). Propitiation is something we do to make someone inclined to be good to us. If we feel we have done something to hurt someone, and we take a gift to that person that makes him feel better toward us: that is propitiation.

God sent His Son as a propitiation to Himself. Because of what Jesus did on Calvary's cross, God is kind to those who put their trust in the Lord Jesus.

Chapter 12

JUSTIFIED BY FAITH

(Romans 3:27-31)

Do you know that you can be forgiven without depending on anything you do in your own efforts?

> Therefore we conclude that a man is justified by faith without the deeds of the law (Rom. 3:28).

In this passage Paul emphasizes that a person can be right with God, because of what God will do for him, in him, and to him, in and through His Son Jesus, apart from any effort or activity on the part of the person himself. Each person is justified by faith, but not because he believes that God gives him free passage to heaven. God does not reward anyone for simply believing, as if believing had some value of its own. God has provided for the person what he needs in Jesus Christ, and that person can receive it from Jesus Christ by yielding to Him in faith and by believing in Him.

When we receive Jesus Christ freely as a gift from God — yielding to Him, obeying Him, and receiving Him the way He is presented in the gospel — God will work in us that which is pleasing in His sight. We will be born again and made right in the sight of God by God Himself. It is like the men in a lifeboat, coming from a sinking ship, getting to shore without swimming. If we believe in the Lord Jesus Christ, God will save us to Himself without our working for it. It is a free gift.

A person riding in an elevator arrives on the tenth floor without taking even one step on the stairs. He does not ride part way in the elevator, then get out and run up a few steps on the stairs, then get back into the elevator again. Once he gets into the elevator he stays there, and it takes him to the tenth floor. When a person trusts in Jesus, putting his full confidence in Him, He will lift that person into the presence of God.

This enables us to understand what Paul is saying in verse 27: "Where is boasting then? It is excluded." Is this because of the person's works, as though his efforts had been adequate? No. It was given freely to him by an operation of faith. Receiving the grace of God as a gift produces what is needed by the grace of God, and as a result the person is humbly grateful to Him. He rejoices in the Lord and thanks Him for His goodness.

> Is he the God of the Jews only? is he not also of the Gentiles? Yes, of the Gentiles also (Rom. 3:29).

Is this not also true for all who believe? Paul is making this point for the Gentiles too. "Whosoever will" may come. Paul would not deny the importance of religious training; however, one could know every other part of the Bible, but if he did not know Jesus Christ he would not be saved.

> Seeing it is one God, which shall justify the circumcision by faith, and uncircumcision through faith. Do we then make void the law through faith? (Rom. 3:30,31).

When we say one can be saved without knowing all that is in the Bible, not having been brought up in a Christian home, are we thereby saying it does not matter what is in the Bible? No, we are emphasizing the very thing the Bible teaches: God will save to the uttermost those who come to Him. If a person has been brought up in a Christian home he will find the way more easily; if he believes, he will be saved despite his upbringing.

"Do we then make void the law through faith?" Are we saying it does not matter if a person broke the law because he is saved by the grace of God? "God forbid: yea, we establish the law." Actually we are confirming what the Bible says.

In Romans 4 we shall see what the Scriptures make plain: all are eligible through Jesus Christ — only through Him.

Remember in the opening chapters of Romans, Paul emphasizes that all have sinned and come short of the glory of God; no one is righteous, and all the world is guilty before God. Now Paul reiterates that everyone can be saved, because Christ Jesus died for all men. "Whosoever will" may come. The Jew? Yes. The Gentile? Yes. Almighty God, who made all men on the face of the earth, sent His only begotten Son for all people, that whosoever believes in Him should not perish but have everlasting life. This is what Paul wants us to remember. It is a free gift, and anyone can have it.

Chapter 13

THE BLESSEDNESS OF SINS FORGIVEN

(Romans 4:1-8)

Can you understand the joy of having all your sins forgiven and taken away by the goodness of God?

> Blessed is the man to whom the Lord will not impute sin (Rom. 4:8).

This Old Testament reference was quoted by the apostle Paul in the New Testament Book of Romans when he was writing about the gospel of Jesus Christ. In this epistle Paul carefully shows how all the world is guilty before God. One may think Paul was a harsh judge, but he was merely revealing truth. Paul no more affected the lives of the people he discussed than a thermometer affects the weather.

Next Paul affirms that salvation has been promised for all men, without obligation. While it was true that there are people who disregard the Scriptures, this does not mean the Bible is not true. Those who pay no attention to the gospel of Jesus Christ do not destroy its validity. Everyone is welcome to receive it, and it will be valid for anyone.

Now, as though such grace were almost too wonderful to believe, Paul uses illustrations from the Old Testament to prove his point. He speaks about Abraham and David, and he could not have chosen two men more impressive for the Jewish people. The promise was made to Abraham, and the covenant was renewed to David. The Lord Jesus is spoken of in the New Testament as being the Son of Abraham and the Son of David.

Paul points out that Abraham was justified by faith.

> For what saith the scripture? Abraham believed God, and it was counted unto him for righteousness (Rom. 4:3).

Abraham walked with God and was counted as a friend of God.

The disposition to walk with God and seek His face did not come through Abraham's own efforts. He understood something about what God would do, and he looked for a city with foundations, whose builder and maker was God. He counted on God keeping His promise.

God had said to Abraham, "Get thee out of thy country, and from thy kindred, and from thy father's house, unto a land that I will show thee" (Gen. 12:1). When we say that Abraham believed, we do not mean that Abraham stayed where he was and believed that he would receive the promise. He actually left the country and went out, not knowing where he was going, following the guidance of God. That is what "believing" means.

Paul says about David, "David also describeth the blessedness of the man, unto whom God imputeth righteousness without works" (Rom. 4:6); that is, God gives it to him. To support this Paul writes:

> Blessed are they whose iniquities are forgiven, and whose sins are covered. Blessed is the man to whom the Lord will not impute sin (Rom. 4:7,8).

Paul is referring to those whose iniquities are forgiven and whose sins are covered, those who put their faith in God. He had pointed out:

> Now to him that worketh is the reward not reckoned of grace, but of debt (Rom. 4:4).

When I earn something I receive fulfillment of an obligation — wages — from an employer. He is not obligated to give me anything I did not earn. But if he gives me money as a gift, I am to receive it on the basis of his goodness, regardless of whether I am strong or weak, or how long I work.

This is Paul's emphasis at this point, and this is blessedness of God that we have when we believe in Him. He has arranged to give us freely all we need for our salvation. We can accept it even though we have not earned it.

Chapter 14

THE PROMISE IS TO ALL

(Romans 4:9-16)

Do you realize the blessing of God is for everyone?

> Therefore it is of faith, that it might be by grace; to the end the promise might be sure to all the seed (Rom. 4:16).

It may seem strange that the gospel, which was given to help make man right in the sight of God, should be equally available to all men, no matter who they are. I suspect almost everyone would think that the activities of the church, the teaching of the gospel, and the preaching of the Bible are supposed to promote righteous living. One might suppose that righteousness would be made the condition of receiving the blessing. But here is the unique feature of the gospel: while it is preached for the purpose of producing people who will be in the likeness of the Lord Jesus Christ and who will walk right with God, it is to be received as a free gift by anyone who believes.

Throughout the history of mankind the tendency has been for people who have lived better lives to claim special favors because they were righteous. If it were a matter of getting our just deserts, it would be true such persons would get more. Because this tendency is found in the natural man, "good" persons are inclined to become vain and proud for they feel they have a great advantage; and this attitude is apt to completely discourage those who know they are far from good. Actually the gospel is free to everyone. Yet this does not mean that everyone will come, and this must also be recognized.

Since the time of Abraham there have always been some who believed in God. They knew about His promises and they dedicated their infants to God; they wanted almighty God to bless and keep them. Many Jews did this. There were in the city where Jesus grew up those who believed in God and who brought up their children in the training of God. It would have been natural to think that the children who grew up in these homes would receive preferred treatment over children living in homes where there was no reference to God; but this was not true. Paul is saying that when that lifeboat comes to bring people from the sinking ship to shore, it will bring both those who can swim and those who cannot swim. This is why anyone who will may come.

Romans 4:9-16 is based on personal facts in the life of Abraham. Paul reasons, "Cometh this blessedness then upon the circumcision only, or upon the uncircumcision also?" (Rom. 4:9a). In other words, are children brought up in religious homes with believing parents the only ones who will be saved? Or is salvation free also for the children who have not been thus trained?

> For we say that faith was reckoned to Abraham for righteousness. How was it then reckoned? when he was in circumcision, or in uncircumcision? (Rom. 4:9,10).

Abraham lived for a length of time as a natural man when he had not been circumcised. Not until after Isaac was born late in his life was the ceremony of circumcision begun. Abraham "believed God, and it was counted unto him for righteousness" long before there was any circumcision. Paul argues then that it must be possible for a man who has not been circumcised to receive the blessing of God because Abraham did. Thus Paul contended that salvation is for everyone, based on the personal facts in the life of Abraham, because he believed in God and was blessed, both before and after he was circumcised.

Therefore, one whose past record is not good can receive the gospel, as well as one whose record is quite good. The gospel is a gift given freely. Later when we discuss the gospel in greater detail we will see that there is always blessing upon righteousness, and that God always blesses those who are obedient to Him.

Chapter 15

FAITH IS NOT HINDERED BY NATURE

(Romans 4:17-25)

Can you understand that a man who believes in God trusts His promises and is influenced very little by the natural situation?

> . . . even God, who quickeneth the dead, and calleth those things which be not as though they were (Rom. 4:17).

In many respects this is a most remarkable description of God. The English word *quicken* means "make alive, sensitive." The word *dead* means "unresponsive." When stimulations do not affect a person, he is dead. The light shines but the dead eye does not see it; sound may be in the room but the dead ear does not hear it; something touches the dead hand but the hand does not feel it. When "quickened," he who is dead is made "alive." That God "quickeneth the dead" means He brings the dead to life.

We should remember God does not quicken all people, because all do not turn to Him. He looks upon every human being and sees what each will potentially be. Almighty God, looking upon me, would see me as what I am one day going to be, not what I am now. He "calleth those things which be not as though they were." I may be a weak believer, but if I have my trust in the Lord Jesus Christ, God deals with me as though I were already in Him, complete and perfect. This is what Abraham did:

> Who against hope believed in hope, that he might become the father of many nations, according to that which was spoken, So shall thy seed be (Rom. 4:18).

Do you remember when that promise was made to Abraham? When God took Abraham out, showed him the stars in the heavens, and asked him to count them, He told him if he could count those stars he would be able to count his seed, which would be as the stars of the heaven in multitude. This had been promised to Abraham before anything happened, and he believed it, "who against hope believed in hope." It was more than could be expected, yet he believed in the promise of God that he would become "the father of many nations, according to that which was spoken, So shall thy seed be."

In verses 19-21 there is a clear statement of what real faith is:

> And being not weak in faith, he considered not his own body now dead, when he was about an hundred years old, neither yet the deadness of Sarah's womb: he staggered not at the promise of God through unbelief; but was strong in faith, giving glory to God; and being fully persuaded that, what he had promised, he was able also to perform (Rom. 4:19-21).

In what sense was this giving glory to God? It was giving God credit for being able to do what He said He would do. "And being fully persuaded that what he had promised, he was able also to perform." Notice what this does *not* say; it was not what was obviously reasonable, natural, and possible. It was what was promised by God. Paul stresses this because, in living here on earth, the natural situation often would discourage our trusting in God, and we could be in despair; however, Paul underscores the fact that if God has promised anything, it will come to pass. We can believe the Word of God even though there is no natural evidence that what God has promised will happen.

The righteousness that was in Abraham was not the consequence of any natural process. His disposition to do the will of God was not the result of education, training or encouraging a person to do and be good. It was something God gave and Abraham learned, and it is the very crux of our faith in the gospel.

> And therefore it was imputed to him for righteousness. Now it was not written for his sake alone, that it was imputed to him; but for us also, to whom it shall be imputed, if we believe on him that raised up Jesus our Lord from the dead; who was delivered for our offences, and was raised again for our justification (Rom. 4:22-25).

In Christ Jesus, through His resurrection, God makes available a new life in believers because of regeneration. This is extremely important — far more so than I can express in words. It is something for us to ponder over. If we have the promise of God, we should believe it. God will keep His Word no matter what the circumstances may be.

Chapter 16

GRACE AND PEACE THROUGH JESUS CHRIST

(Romans 5:1-2)

Can you understand the importance of what a Christian receives from Jesus Christ after he has peace with God through believing?

I suspect many of us have the feeling that the gospel primarily deals with our getting right with God. We know from our own experience that before we knew the Lord Jesus we realized we were sinners, alienated from God. Because we were sinners we had the experience of being reconciled to God and being accepted by Him. The apostle Paul points out there is much more in the whole truth than just the matter of coming to God. "All have come short of the glory of God." Paul also showed that the work of Christ on Calvary's cross, dying for us and being raised from the dead to reconcile us to God, was done as a free gift. The benefits are received by faith. We will see that believing in Him is more than mentally assenting to the facts, accepting them as true: the actual believing is taking from Him that which is prepared for us in Christ Jesus.

In Romans 5 we find something important about God's plan in Christ. In the first two verses we have a concise picture of the entire work of salvation:

> Therefore being justified by faith, we have peace with God through our Lord Jesus Christ: by whom also we have access by faith into this grace wherein we stand, and rejoice in hope of the glory of God (Rom. 5:1,2).

Many people close the book right there and thank the Lord. Truly what has been described is a glorious thing, but we must not shut the book too soon. "By whom also": The word *also* signifies that just as though having finished and come to the end of one corridor, having peace with God, we turn to the right, and there is a new corridor open to us, a new opportunity. ". . . we have access by faith into this grace wherein we stand, and rejoice in hope of the glory of God." It is possible to have the blessing of God upon us, being justified by faith, and this will never be reduced in any way. In a certain sense something was done on Calvary's cross once and for all. When Jesus died He said, "It is finished." So far as our guilt is concerned, He paid the ransom price; and when He died on the cross, we were set free.

Because Christ Jesus died for us, we have peace about our sins. They were real, but they have been expiated. We have been redeemed from guilt. We will not be judged as to whether He will accept us: that has been settled. But even though our sins have all been forgiven, we still have within us the disposition to sin, which is embarrassing, humiliating, and many times degrading. We are delivered from this sin by faith in the death of Jesus Christ. We need not be subject to the evil tendencies that are within us by our natures. Paul shows that we can be set free from the dominance of sin in our members; and because we are free from them, we can have peace and confidence with God. If God did not spare His only Son but freely gave Him up for us all, "how shall he not with him also freely give us all things?" (Rom. 8:32). He has purchased us with His own blood and He will keep us. We can be content; our futures are secure in Christ Jesus. Do not think that we have peace with God because we are good enough. That is not true. But *He* is good, kind, and gracious enough, and He has opened the door; therefore we have peace with Him.

Now let us look at the second verse which opens the way into endless possibilities: "By whom also we have access by faith into this grace wherein we stand." When thinking of all God has done for us in Christ, we must say *also*. There is more. There are certain privileges open to us; in the performance of believing we will come into this grace wherein we stand. ". . . and rejoice in hope of the glory of God."

The word *glory* always suggests the harvest idea of fruit. "In this is my Father glorified, that you bear much fruit." When Paul rejoiced in the hope of the glory of God, he was rejoicing in the hope that God would produce fruit in him by His grace in Jesus Christ.

Chapter 17

THE LOVE OF GOD

(Romans 5:3-8)

Do you think the love of God is reserved only for believers?

> But God commendeth his love toward us, in that, while we were yet sinners, Christ died for us (Rom. 5:8).

Over and over again, when reading the Bible, my heart warms within me when I come to this verse, because it is so close to my own personal experience. When I was thinking about the gospel of the Lord Jesus Christ and considering becoming a Christian, I suddenly realized that if the Lord God and I were ever going to get together He would have to bridge the gap. I didn't know where He was, and I didn't know how to get to Him. I was like a blind person, a lost sheep. My heart sank at the thought that He would have to come to me. I had previously tried to do all the right things but I had no confidence in myself; I knew that God knew me better than I knew myself, and I could scarcely believe He would put Himself out to come to me. That is why this verse means so much to me.

As Paul explains the riches of the grace of God that we have in Christ Jesus, he tells us that God watches over us after we believe in Christ, even to the forgiveness of sin and the removal of guilt. When we accept Jesus, our guilt is removed, but this is not the end of it: God continues to watch over us, leading us further and further into blessing. In our next study we will see more about the glory of God in removing wrath. Paul emphasizes the amazing truth that God will do good to us even when we are not obedient. Being forgiven is a wonderful thing: we can now come into the presence of God and ask for help in living. Now let us think carefully through verses 3-5:

> And not only so, but we glory in tribulations also: knowing that

> tribulation worketh patience; and patience, experience; and experience, hope: and hope maketh not ashamed; because the love of God is shed abroad in our hearts by the Holy Ghost which is given unto us.

Paul is saying that we have high hopes of results — we expect good consequences to be derived from tribulations. While trouble itself does not produce patience (not everyone who has trouble will be patient), if we have the patience of the love of God within us because we trust Him, then tribulation actually brings out this patience. And patience works in experience. Patience means placing our hands in God's hand and walking with Him regardless of the trouble we are having.

As we have this experience with God, we become more and more confident of what He will do, because we see Him working things out for our good. Hope keeps us going to the end results, and we will never be embarrassed because of lack of consequences. If we hope in God we will continue to walk with Him, and He will eventually show us His will. This will all happen because the love of God is shed abroad in our hearts by the Holy Spirit. In all our trouble and patience, in all experience and hope, there are certain things about the Lord Jesus that will never leave our minds. The Holy Spirit will show us how Christ died for us. He will remind us that Jesus went to the cross on our behalf, and that He rose from the dead and now prays in heaven on our behalf.

This is how Paul argues: "For when we were yet without strength, in due time Christ died for the ungodly" (5:6). He started it. This encourages us to believe in Him. "For scarcely for a righteous man will one die: yet peradventure for a good man some would even dare to die. But God commendeth his love toward us, in that, while we were yet sinners, Christ died for us" (5:7,8).

At this point Paul would say, "Praise the Lord!" He cannot get over the fact that regardless of how much trouble he has experienced, the Holy Spirit shows him that Jesus died for him and God really cares about him. And God really cares about you.

Chapter 18

SAVED FROM WRATH

(Romans 5:9-11)

Do you think God would ever deal in wrath with anyone?

> Much more then, being now justified by his blood, we shall be saved from wrath through him (Rom. 5:9).

There is more to being saved than being forgiven our sins. Perhaps we should say that being forgiven involves more than escape from destruction. The word *wrath* is commonly understood to be a manifestation of hot anger or cold rage, as the case may be. When we think of a person's being filled with wrath, we are inclined to think that this is something harsh, forbidding, threatening violence. But when Paul uses the word he means something that occurs quite often.

The words *wrath* and *glory* have something in common in addition to the fact they refer to what will happen in eternity: those who are under the wrath of God will be destroyed; those who are in the glory of God will be saved forever. These words also refer to a contemporary aspect of life. There is a manifestation of glory as well as a manifestation of the wrath of God that takes place in everyday affairs.

In John 15, while speaking of these things to His disciples, the Lord Jesus said, "Herein is my Father glorified, that ye bear much fruit" (v. 8). A disciple's bearing fruit was manifesting the glory of God. Just as glory can be seen in this world, so also is wrath seen. As it occurs in Scripture, the word *glory* in Hebrew is largely associated with harvest time, which indicates the fulfillment of potential. It is when the wheat produces bushels of grain that we see the glory of the wheat field; it is when the apple tree produces barrels of apples that we see the glory of the apple tree. This is the way the word *glory* is ordinarily used in Scripture. The word *blessing* leads up to glory, and the word *cursing* belongs in the same vocabulary. God will curse just as He will bless.

The curse of God and the blessing of God are similar in operation. If a person plants one bushel of wheat and reaps a harvest of twenty bushels, he has nineteen extra bushels. Those nineteen bushels are blessing, and we would properly say that God blessed the farmer. Suppose a weed grows in someone's garden and is allowed to mature and go to seed, so that in the next season twenty weeds have grown. For this we use the word *cursing*. The nineteen extra desirable bushels of wheat are blessings and the nineteen extra undesirable weeds are cursing. All the blessing taken together we call "glory" and all the cursing taken together we call "wrath." We speak of the wrath of God not as God arbitrarily acting out of His spite to anyone, but something which comes as a consequence of evil that is done. "Whatsoever a man soweth, that shall he also reap." If he sows to the flesh, he shall of the flesh reap corruption (cursing). If he sows to the spirit, he shall of the spirit reap life everlasting (blessing).

The wrath of God is described in the first chapter of Romans: "For the wrath of God is revealed from heaven against all ungodliness and unrighteousness of men" (v. 18). God's wrath comes from heaven, but it is revealed on earth. In verse 24 we read that God gave certain people up to uncleanness: this is part of the wrath of God.

> And changed the glory of the uncorruptible God into an image made like to corruptible man. . . . Wherefore God also gave them up to uncleanness (Rom. 1:23,24).

The vile affections that developed among those people were consequences of changing the truth of God into a lie. God allowed the wrong they did to develop into more wrong. We may be dismayed at this, because from time to time some of us will sow that which is wrong. But God is faithful and He will do for us more than we can ask or think: this is what Paul refers to here.

> Much more then, being now justified by his blood, we shall be saved from wrath through him (Rom. 5:9).

We will be saved from the consequences of our wrongdoing; God will help us keep the weeds down.

Weeds will not produce more weeds in the believer because Christ Jesus is working to deliver him from his sin:

> For if, when we were enemies, we were reconciled to God by the death of his Son, much more, being reconciled, we shall be saved by his life (Rom. 5:10).

We will be saved not by His life on earth (those thirty-three years He lived as Jesus of Nazareth), but His life now in the presence of God, where He intercedes on our behalf before God.

This is what Paul is confident about. Christ is able to save to the uttermost those who come unto God by Him.

Chapter 19

GRACE IS FREE

(Romans 5:12-18)

Do you realize that much that affects us, both for bad and good, exists within us?

In Romans 5:12-18 we have a truth set forth which is commonly unknown but which affects believers on every side. It is usually not recognized, even when it has been heard, because it is difficult to understand and perhaps even more difficult to believe. There is one basic principle behind all that is written here: No man is alone, left to his own desires.

There is a simple analysis of this truth presented by the apostle Paul. Scripture indicates that all human beings, descendants of Adam, have within them the sinful life of Adam. We feel sentimentally and compassionately drawn to babies in their helplessness and innocence. They do not know what is going on, nor do they know what they have done or what they are doing. Because of this it is easy for us to think they have in them nothing evil. As far as being responsible for what they do, of course they are not responsible. But we need to recognize that the life in them is the life of Adam — prone to selfishness and wrongdoing and the disposition to look out for self. Because babies are human, it is natural for them to act this way. This is part of their heritage from Adam.

Paul argues that it is the same with Christ. When a person is born again, the very life of Christ is in him and will naturally turn him to God, with the desire to please God at all times. This is something given by the grace of God when any person receives Jesus Christ as Savior. It is the new life in the believer that leads him through his own Gethsemane, to his own Calvary, into the resurrection life, and into real communion with God. Paul points out that in Christ every believer is included in

His obedience and in His faith in God, as in His very nature.

In the King James Version of the Bible Romans 5:13-17 is put in parentheses, which means these verses compose one line of thought. A person can read verse 12 and then verse 18 straight through as one thought, then afterward read verses 13 to 17.

> Wherefore, as by one man sin entered into the world, and death by sin; and so death passed upon all men, for that all have sinned. . . . Therefore, as by the offence of one judgment came upon all men to condemnation; even so by the righteousness of one the free gift came upon all men unto justification of life (Rom. 5:12,18).

In Adam all the children of Adam actually partook of his nature. Just as he turned to sin, they will all turn to sin. But in Christ Jesus, as He was disposed to obey the Father, so all those who are in Christ Jesus will be inwardly directed to obey the Father. Verses 13-17 discuss this whole matter: "For until the law sin was in the world." From the time of Adam until the time of Moses men did not have the Ten Commandments; but what was right was right and what was wrong was wrong, even if they did not have the commandments.

To illustrate, a man bought a farm consisting of 160 acres of land, around which there was no fence. Five years afterward he put a fence around it. Putting up the fence did not make it his land — it was his land all the time — but putting the fence around it showed the limits of his property. So it is with the law: the law does not make anything right or wrong; it simply states what is right and what is wrong. It puts up a fence where the boundary line actually is. ". . . but sin is not imputed when there is no law." You would not condemn anyone for driving into the other man's field if there were no fence to warn him. "Nevertheless death reigned from Adam to Moses, even over them that had not sinned after the similitude of Adam's transgression, who is the figure of him that was to come." This is saying that death reigned from Adam to Moses even if the individual people, children of Adam, did not do the same wrong thing that Adam did. Even so, the life that was in them was sentenced to death. "But not as the offence, so also is the free gift." We will find that the free gift is more wonderful than the offense was. "For if through the offence of one [that is, Adam] many be dead, much more the grace of God, and the gift by grace, which is by one man, Jesus Christ, hath abounded unto many [to all those who are born again and are in Him]. And not as it was by one that sinned, so is the gift: for the judgment was by one to condemnation, but the free gift is of many offences unto justification" (Rom. 5:15,16).

Basically, Adam did one thing wrong and we were condemned. But when we are in Christ we are justified not just about one thing, but about everything. "For if by one man's offence death reigned by one; much more they which receive abundance of grace and of the gift of righteousness shall reign in life by one, Jesus Christ" (Rom. 5:17).

This is what Paul is saying: Every human being descended from Adam has sin in him, and he will sin just as naturally as he breathes. Every born-again Christian will have in him the will to turn to God, just as flowers turn their faces to the sun, and the disposition to want to do the will of God. This is the new life that is in Christ Jesus, and both are in the Christian.

Chapter 20

GRACE IS ABUNDANT

(Romans 5:19-21)

Have you understood that grace is greater than all our sins?

It would be easy to form the impression that, because we say the gospel of the Lord Jesus Christ is for everyone and that He died for all men, all men will inherit grace simply because they are human beings. But this is not true. Remember that the gospel is for all men, the children of Adam; but it is effectual only for those who believe in Jesus Christ. The promise is to everyone but the truth will become valid only in those who believe.

How about the person who doesn't believe? It is a challenging truth that the children of Adam and the children of God are not the same group of people. The children of Adam, as the phrase indicates, are born of human beings biologically, and they are descendants of the first man. The children of God are spiritually begotten of God as they believe in the gospel. We could wish that all the children of Adam believed all the Word of God, but this is not the way it is. Only those who believe are born again.

It is a glorious truth that any child of Adam — any human being — can accept Christ as Savior. But it must be soberly remembered that only those who come are to be counted as the ones who will receive the blessing. "Whosoever will" may come but "whosoever believeth not" is condemned already. Let me say again: as a human being I am a sinner not so much by choice but because I was born that way. As a believer I am a child of God, not because every day in every situation I always do God's will; I am a child of God because I believe in the Lord Jesus Christ. There is given to me a new life; and this new life in me in its inherent nature moves me to want to do the will of

God. In the sense that Adam is responsible for my wanting to sin, when I am in Christ and trusting in Him, it is Christ Jesus who is responsible for my inner disposition to be holy, to obey God.

> For as by one man's disobedience many were made sinners, so by the obedience of one shall many be made righteous (Rom. 5:19).

There may be people who think it is not fair that they were not created angels, that God allowed them to be born sinful human beings. But actually it is also not fair that any of us should be saved. It is not fair that we should be heirs of God and joint heirs of Jesus Christ. We have not earned it. In this whole situation, it is not a matter of being fair. When we were in Adam we inherited the nature of Adam; when we are in Christ we inherit the nature of Christ. We need to remember: God was so concerned about our condition in Adam He sent His only begotten Son to give us this opportunity, and anyone who has heard the gospel can settle it once and for all by giving himself over to God in Christ Jesus and having the blessing of God.

> Moreover the law entered, that the offence might abound (Rom. 5:20).

This verse says that the truth was in Adam as it is in Christ. It did not change with the giving of the commandments to Moses. It was always wrong to steal; it was always wrong to kill. When Cain killed Abel, that was wrong. Moses had not yet lived and the Ten Commandments were not yet given until hundreds of years later, but it was wrong from the first for one man to kill another. "But where sin abounded, grace did much more abound." This is a wonderful truth that we shall study in chapters 6 through 8.

Chapter 21

DEATH IS INCLUDED IN OUR FAITH

(Romans 6:1-7)

Do you know that when a person is a believer it involves counting part of himself to be dead?

In chapters 6 and 7 we will come to some difficult passages in which Paul discusses aspects of believing which we cannot always see and which most people are not aware of. This discussion could not be carried on in any ordinary situation, like the usual classroom in a university, and be fully understood. Paul uses specialized vocabulary, which it is necessary to understand if the meaning is to be grasped. If our hearts are right with God, we will benefit by this discussion.

Paul has just emphasized the truth about Adam and about Christ. In Adam, all human beings derive their life. Adam was created in the flesh, and whatever is born of the flesh is flesh. With reference to Christ Jesus, it is true that he that is born of the spirit is spirit. Those who believe in the gospel and accept the Lord Jesus are, by the grace of God, regenerated. They will have the new nature in them — the nature of the Lord Jesus Christ. Paul points out the believer is involved in both of these relationships, although they are contrary to each other. The disposition in the flesh is to be selfish; the disposition in the spirit is to be godly.

Paul closed chapter 5 with the confident statement that grace is greater than sin: "where sin aboundeth, grace does much more abound" (Rom. 5:20). Someone may say that since sin abounds and grace even more abounds, believers can sin all they may want, and yet be saved. Paul considers this problem. He does not argue the merits of this issue from logic to point out the unreasonableness of it; he cuts the ground from under it by what he understands to be the meaning of faith. Paul points out that if a person believes in Jesus Christ, he is already doing something about his flesh: he is counting it dead. When he counts his flesh dead, he will not act in the flesh any more. The problem would never arise because when a person believes in Christ Jesus, he is believing his flesh into death. These words may seem strange, but they will become clearer as the reader follows Paul's argument.

> What shall we say then? Shall we continue in sin, that grace may abound? God forbid. How shall we, that are dead to sin, live any longer therein? (Rom. 6:1,2).

In verse 2 he is asking if the believer has already taken his flesh into death so that his flesh is no longer independent, doing as it pleases. After that how could he sin deliberately? The question is artificial, for it is not possible.

> Know ye not, that so many of us as were baptized into Jesus Christ were baptized into his death? (Rom. 6:3).

This is an important point. If the believer has been baptized into Jesus Christ, he may have celebrated it with public baptism. When he did this he claimed that he was baptized into Christ's death. Just as Christ took His body to the cross, so the believer brings his body to the cross.

> Therefore we are buried with him by baptism into death: that like as Christ was raised up from the dead by the glory of the Father, even so we also should walk in newness of life (Rom. 6:4).

God's plan is that when the soul believes in and trusts in the Lord Jesus Christ, this involves following Him. Christ yielded Himself and died; believers also yield themselves and die. God raised Christ from the dead, and God will raise believers from the dead. Therein will be their salvation.

> For if we have been planted together in the likeness of his death, we shall be also in the likeness of his resurrection (Rom. 6:5).

If by believing Christians yield themselves to God's will so that they will follow Jesus in His ministry and life, even to the point of being denied and rejected by everyone else, they will be also in the likeness of His resurrection. They can count on that happening to them just as it did to Him.

> Knowing this, that our old man is crucified with him, that the

> body of sin might be destroyed, that henceforth we should not serve sin (Rom. 6:6).

This is God's way of salvation. The old man — the natural person, the child of Adam — is crucified with Christ. When anyone believes in Christ he accepts the idea that he himself is dead "that the body of sin might be destroyed." Paul indicates that one of the believer's problems is that the flesh which is with him in the body cannot in itself ever do the things that are pleasing to God. Thus having this body the believer might ask how he can ever be free from it. Paul points out that Jesus died in the flesh so the believer could see what to do with his human nature — he must yield it to God: "That the body of sin might be destroyed, that henceforth we should not serve sin. For he that is dead is freed from sin" (Rom. 6:6,7).

Chapter 22

DEAD BUT ALIVE

(Romans 6:8-11)

Have you ever thought about what it means to say, "I am dead"?

> Likewise reckon ye also yourselves to be dead indeed unto sin, but alive unto God through Jesus Christ our Lord (Rom. 6:11).

In this section the apostle Paul continues his discussion about what takes place within a believer, who has in him both the old man of the flesh and the new man of Christ Jesus. Being born in this world as a human being, he is a child of Adam; but because he believes the gospel and has accepted Christ, he is a child of God. Now he must make choices between the two. Paul discusses this and undertakes to show what takes place.

The gospel of Jesus Christ has one main purpose with regard to sin, and this is actually what the gospel is all about. The gospel offers to redeem the believer from sin in a valid procedure so that no one can object. Paul reveals this by showing the reality of the death of Christ for believers. He redeems them from sin. After that, Paul shows how they can definitely be delivered from sin by showing the reality of flesh and spirit. By "flesh" Paul means everything a person receives in his natural life from his parents, his community, and his experience as a human being. When he speaks of "spirit" he is referring to the new nature that is in the believer because he believes in the Lord Jesus Christ through the gospel.

Both flesh (biologically derived from father and mother) and spirit (which comes spiritually from the Word of God which has been heard as preached) have their own processes. They are different. The flesh eats, drinks, works, and has interests of its own; the spirit also eats, drinks, and has interests of its own; but the interests of the spirit and the flesh are not identical. Often they are contrary to one another.

As an illustration let us think about holding a knife in our hand. If we open our hand and let it go, what will happen? The knife will drop. Why? Because the knife in itself has weight, which, in response to gravitation, pulls it down. If we lift the hand clasping the knife, the knife will rise; if we swing it to the right or left, the knife will move also. The knife has weight and is always ready to fall. It does not fall and actually serves us, because we are holding it. In itself the knife could never do anything but fall; however, in our hand it can do whatever we desire. Even so it is with our flesh.

Each person is born first in the flesh, and as a person he can be regenerated in Christ Jesus. The flesh is prone to sin, but the believer is prone to obey God. Paul uses the work of Christ's dying on Calvary, and being raised in the Resurrection, to point out what can happen when the Christian has been delivered from the deadness of his soul. The flesh can be reckoned dead, but the spirit is alive. Temptation cannot appeal to the dead person (the flesh). Therefore the believer can be free from temptation because his flesh is reckoned dead, yet his spirit is alive unto Christ Jesus. This is a practical description of what it means to believe.

> Now if we be dead with Christ, we believe that we shall also live with him: knowing that Christ being raised from the dead dieth no more; death hath no more dominion over him (Rom. 6:8,9).

This is a wonderful promise because, having been through the experience of death, it will not come a second time. If we have believed in Christ in the course of His death, we will be brought into His resurrection life never to die again.

> Death hath no more dominion over him. For in that he died, he died unto sin once: but in that he liveth, he liveth unto God. Likewise reckon ye also yourselves to be dead indeed unto sin, but alive unto God through Jesus Christ our Lord (Rom. 6:9-11).

If you count yourself to be dead, things that ordinarily disturb you will no longer do so. For instance, if an acquaintance does not recognize you and walks past without speaking, you might feel resentment. But if you counted yourself a dead person, what difference would it make to a dead person if he was not spoken to? A person who reckons himself dead is free from wrath and things of that nature.

I should like to point out that if we are not dead with Christ, we shall not live with Him. That is one of the problems in Christian experience in the church. Many of us want all the blessings of the gospel, but we do not want to go through the experience of the gospel. We must be willing to give up other things and remember that God is preparing something for us that will be more than what we are giving up. We are alive, but we must count ourselves as if we were dead. God will then raise us from the dead in the newness of life.

Chapter 23

YIELDING TO GOD

(Romans 6:12-16)

If you reckon yourself to be dead, can you see that you are actually yielding yourself to the will of God?

> Let not sin therefore reign in your mortal body, that ye should obey it in the lusts thereof (Rom. 6:12).

Paul is describing in this chapter what is involved in yielding oneself to the will of God and being lifted into doing His will. It seems strange to say we give ourselves to God so that we can actually get something done. When we yield ourselves to God in the Lord Jesus Christ, accepting what He has done for us as a pattern, we make it possible for God to do things in and through us that will bring salvation. A man can cross a lake without swimming or rowing by letting the motor on the boat take him over, and one can get to the tenth floor of a building without climbing stairs simply by getting into an elevator and letting it lift him. Something similar is the picture in mind here: "Let not sin therefore reign in your mortal body, that ye should obey it in the lusts thereof."

You will not be using your mortal body anymore; that is, you will not depend on it. You have reckoned yourself dead and God is raising you from the dead. You can have a victorious attitude toward sin in your mortal body. How would sin be in your mortal body? Sin is born there and as long as you draw breath in your physical body you will have the disposition to selfishness and self-indulgence. But when you reckon the body to be dead, you act as though your natural life is dead. Then sin cannot bind you because the flesh is dead. Although sin may entice you, you will not respond — a dead man doesn't care. "Let not sin therefore reign." The sin is in your members, but you need not let it control you because you are free from it.

> Neither yield ye your members as instruments of unrighteousness unto sin (Rom. 6:13).

You need not do for yourself what is suggested by your body. You do not have to eat or drink what looks good, nor do you have to touch what looks good to touch if you reckon yourself dead.

> For sin shall not have dominion over you; for ye are not under the law, but under grace (Rom. 6:14).

This statement could be easily misunderstood. The reason you are free is that sin worked in the flesh and the flesh is reckoned dead. You are alive in the spirit, which is stronger than the flesh. The temptation which comes out of the flesh is coming now to a dead body. Since this is the case, when you are born again and you have the new life in you, sin will not have dominion over you. This is true when you are raised from the dead and are under grace. You are dependent upon the spirit.

> What then? shall we sin, because we are not under the law, but under grace? (Rom. 6:15).

Actually you will not want to sin because you are counting the body to be dead.

> Know ye not, that to whom ye yield yourselves servants to obey, his servants ye are to whom ye obey; whether of sin unto death, or of obedience unto righteousness? (Rom. 6:16).

Notice those last two words: *sin* and *obedience*. So far as your flesh is concerned, the tendency is to do what pleases you, and this is sin — self-indulgence — the opposite of which is obedience — doing what God wants you to do.

This is how it is in the spirit, and this is how it is in Christ Jesus. Obedience is what God produces as we put our trust in Him.

Chapter 24

SERVANTS OF GOD ARE FREE FROM SIN

(Romans 6:17-21)

Do you realize that a believer never has the problem of deciding what to do, as others may think he has?

> Being then made free from sin, ye became the servants of righteousness (Rom. 6:18).

Much more is involved in becoming a Christian than most people realize. One way we can tell that someone has started to live the life of faith is that he joins the church or makes an open profession of faith. We may think that now he will try to be a better person. But this idea does not reflect what is actually happening, because while people often think that becoming a believer is a matter of deciding to act differently, this is not really the way it is. Believing is not primarily a matter of doing right. Believing is a matter of being committed to, sharing with, and being in communion with the living Lord Jesus Christ. Believing the gospel is a matter of yielding to the living Lord and letting Him strengthen and lead us.

Here again, the basic element is yielding oneself — heart, mind, and strength — to God in and through Christ Jesus. You may remember that in the Sermon on the Mount Jesus of Nazareth said, "No man can serve two masters." It is often easy for us to think that if we were only free from sin we would do very well. There is no such thing as being in a vacuum; no one is ever entirely free. Either we will do the things that please ourselves, or we will do what pleases the Lord Jesus. There is no such thing as being free from sin and then being neutral. No, you come out of one into the other. You are either dead or alive, not halfway between.

Paul discusses this in Romans 6:17: "But God be thanked, that ye were the servants of sin, but ye have obeyed from the heart that form of doctrine which was delivered you." You used to yield yourself to act as you pleased, which was sinful. Now instead of doing what you want to do, you yield yourself to the indwelling Lord Jesus Christ and allow Him to guide your actions. Many think that being a believer means that either you do what you want to do, which is wrong; or you do what Christ wants you to do, which is right. It is better stated that first you yield yourself to the Lord, and then He moves you to do His will.

The first thing Christ wants you to do is to yield yourself to Him. He stands with His hand outstretched; put your hand in His and walk with Him. That is the form of doctrine that "was delivered unto you." You were not given instructions on how to perform good deeds; you were instructed how to walk with the Lord. Don't ever forget that. Living the life of faith is learning how to have Christ with you in every facet of your life. This is the gospel of the Lord Jesus Christ. "Being then made free from sin. . . ." As pointed out earlier, this means being free from sin by dying in the flesh when you reckoned your human nature to be dead so that sin could not move through your dead human nature. ". . . ye became the servants of righteousness." This is the phrase used to describe those who are yielded to the living Lord. That person is righteous.

> I speak after the manner of men because of the infirmity of your flesh: for as ye have yielded your members servants to uncleanness and to iniquity unto iniquity; even so now yield your members to righteousness unto holiness (Rom. 6:19).

You once yielded your body to do what you wanted to do; then you were the servant of sin, and you were free from righteousness. But now it is the other way around. Paul says, "What fruit had ye then in those things whereof ye are now ashamed? for the end of those things is death" (Rom. 6:21). Here Paul is appealing to common sense. There is no such thing as being neutral in this battle of the soul. Either you walk with yourself or you walk with the Lord: no man can serve two masters. If you prefer to belong to the Lord and be godly in Christ Jesus, Paul would say, let's make a go of it. Let's really commit ourselves to it.

Chapter 25

THE GIFT OF GOD

(Romans 6:22,23)

Have you understood that holiness is to be expected as a normal result of real faith?

> For the wages of sin is death; but the gift of God is eternal life through Jesus Christ our Lord (Rom. 6:23).

The whole truth in the gospel is presented in this simple statement. After all, it is a matter of death or life. This should be clear to everyone, yet there is one aspect of this that needs to be pointed out, inasmuch as it is easy to fall into a frame of mind we should be careful to avoid. The wages of sin is death now, not after life is ended and the score added up. Those who live in sin are at the present time living in a state of death. They are dead in trespasses and sin. But also, and perhaps far more gloriously, the free gift of God is eternal life *now*.

Certainly things will be happening in the days to come for those who believe in the Lord Jesus Christ, but there will only be a future if there is a present. Let us look at the two words *death* and *life*. When a body is dead, it is insensitive to its environment and its members deteriorate. This is the significance of death, and so it is with any person who walks away from God. But when a body is alive, it is sensitive to sound, light, touch, and taste. It is responsive. In his first epistle, John speaks of it this way, "He that hath the Son hath life; and He that hath not the Son of God hath not life" (5:12). This is what Paul is emphasizing at this point.

This is not a case of man's soul facing two choices — to live or to die. The truth is, man is in distress now. He will not decide whether one day he will be dead. He is dead now! The question is whether he will live, whether he will turn to God. Paul has carefully outlined his analysis of the situation in this first part of

Romans. The sentence of death is over the whole world and all men are in sin. But in the gospel of God a person can live through Christ Jesus.

As a servant of God "ye have your fruit unto holiness, and the end everlasting life. For the wages of sin is death; but the gift of God is eternal life through Jesus Christ our Lord" (Rom. 6: 22,23).

Chapter 26

FREE FROM THE LAW

(Romans 7:1-6)

Do you understand how death can cancel a legal requirement?

> But now we are delivered from the law, that being dead wherein we were held; that we should serve in newness of spirit, and not in the oldness of the letter (Rom. 7:6).

Here Paul discusses the function and the operation of sin and the law in our experience. He argues that a person can actually be set free from an obligation because of death. Of course, the point he is arriving at was mentioned in the sixth chapter where Paul emphasized the way the Lord Jesus Christ delivers us — by leading us to consider ourselves dead, because when we are dead we are free from the operation of sin in our physical bodies. Paul now argues this from the view of the legal involvement.

It is not easy to keep all of this in mind at one time. Paul uses the illustration of the legal obligation of marriage:

> For the woman which hath an husband is bound by the law to her husband so long as he liveth; but if the husband be dead, she is loosed from the law of her husband (Rom. 7:2).

When a woman's husband dies, she is free to marry another. Suppose a woman's husband is in the armed forces overseas; perhaps they have been separated for several years. If she should marry another man, the law would say she had committed bigamy. However, if her husband died even one minute before she married another, she would not be doing wrong legally; she would be free.

Paul uses this to illustrate an aspect of spiritual experience. The truth he is presenting is far more profound, although the surface pattern is the same. For instance, I am joined to my human body in a vital union, and when my body sins I am guilty because I am involved. As long as my body is alive, I am obligated to pay for the sin that my body commits. But if my body were dead I would no longer be obligated to pay for what my body had done wrong. My spirit would now be free and could be joined to Christ Jesus, so I could be related to Him the way I had previously been related to my body. I would no longer be involved in the sinful desires of my human body; I could now belong to another.

> Wherefore, my brethren, ye also are become dead to the law by the body of Christ; that ye should be married to another, even to him who is raised from the dead, that we should bring forth fruit unto God (Rom. 7:4).

"Ye also are become dead to the law by the body of Christ." We do this by joining with Christ in faith. Remember, He took His body to Calvary's cross, and when we believe in Him we participate in His death on Calvary. Now we consider our flesh, our own human nature, to be like Christ's body — dead. ". . . that ye should be married to another, even to him who is raised from the dead." We now join with the resurrected Christ as Lord that we should "bring forth fruit unto God." Paul is arguing here on the basis of a woman in her marriage relationship, thereby illustrating what happens to us in our spiritual relationship with God.

> For when we were in the flesh, the motions of sins, which were by the law, did work in our members to bring forth fruit unto death (Rom. 7:5).

That is, while we were still living as human beings, the processes of human conduct within us, which operated according to "whatsoever a man soweth that shall he also reap," resulted in death as a natural consequence.

> But now we are delivered from the law, that being dead wherein we were held; that we should serve in newness of spirit, and not in the oldness of the letter (Rom. 7:6).

We are now delivered from the law, by counting the body dead — not because God says He will make different rules and not because we believe that in Christ everything will be done differently, but because in His death Christ has set us free.

When we reckon the body to be dead because we believe in the Lord Jesus Christ, we are set free from the inward workings of sin in our body. We no longer need to reap what we have sown, but we will be able to receive what God gives. We live in a new arrangement where the answer is given by the grace of God: "that we should serve in newness of spirit, and not in the oldness of the letter."

The following six verses present a rather difficult line of thought in which Paul continues to emphasize the importance of counting self dead. He states that the way out of the bondage of sin is the way of the cross. Something happens to us when we believe in Jesus Christ that will issue in our being able to reckon ourselves dead, with the result that the desires and impulses in our hearts and souls will originate in the will of Christ Jesus and will emerge in our consciousness through the presence of Christ. As I trust in Him, He will affect me, and I will find myself being lifted into the will of God.

Chapter 27

SIN IS GREATER BECAUSE OF THE LAW

(Romans 7:7-13)

Can you see that driving too fast might be wrong, but exceeding the speed limit when signs are posted would be worse?

> . . . that sin by the commandment might become exceeding sinful (Rom. 7:13).

Here Paul discusses the condition of sin in the experience of man. We know that sin exists in every person, but Paul stresses that all persons are not alike. Some know more about what they do than others, and this makes them more responsible. For instance, when I park my car I should be thoughtful about parking in front of a neighbor's house. If he should post a No Parking sign, it would be worse to park there. I should be careful about not walking on another's lawn, but if there is a sign that reads Keep Off the Grass, that should prevent me altogether from doing so. After it has been made clear what is right and what is wrong, it is worse when we do wrong. The law gives us a definite pattern. Paul says:

> What shall we say then? Is the law sin? God forbid. Nay, I had not known sin, but by the law: for I had not known lust, except the law had said, Thou shalt not covet (Rom. 7:7).

The law makes clear by revelation to our hearts and minds what is true. "But sin, taking occasion by the commandment, wrought [worked] in me all manner of concupiscence. For without the law sin was dead" (Rom. 7:8). This seems to indicate that when Paul once learned what was right and wrong, he found himself actually wanting to do what was wrong, even though he knew it was wrong. When he did not have the law, sin was dead, perhaps in the sense that sin was dormant. It did not affect him.

> For I was alive without the law once: but when the commandment came, sin revived, and I died (Rom. 7:9).

"For I was alive without the law once" is a way of saying, "When I didn't know right from wrong, I didn't feel wrong." But when he became conscious of what was right and wrong, then sin loomed in his mind. He felt guilty about it, and he died.

> And the commandment, which was ordained to life, I found to be unto death (Rom. 7:10).

The commandment was given to guide people into blessing, but it had become a means of measuring right and wrong. Thus it "measured" Paul and showed him he was wrong.

> For sin, taking occasion by the commandment, deceived me, and by it slew me (Rom. 7:11).

Paul seems to imply that while he was ignorant, unsure of what was right and wrong, he was innocent. But once he knew the law he was guilty before God when he did wrong, because he knew better. The law defines sin in action and tells what is right and what is wrong. So Paul asks if the law made him sin. He replies that it only showed him how sinful he was. According to verse 13, ". . . that sin by the commandment might become exceeding sinful," the law shows us just how wrong sin is.

This fits in with what Paul would tell the Jews, that the law would help them to know in which areas they sinned and how much. This would not help them to do right, but it would show them right from wrong. Then they would be all the more responsible because they had not done right. This is not an easy line of discussion but it belongs within the overall picture. The law is like a curbstone along the side of a street. If you go over it, you will be on someone else's property. The law functions as a curbstone, not the pavement. You do not drive on the curbstone, you drive on the pavement.

The apostle Paul claims that the law — the Ten Commandments — was good for the Jewish people to have, because it showed them what was right and what was wrong. He points out, however, that those Ten Commandments did not have the power to make them do right: they were only guidelines. If you want to do the will of God the law will help you, but if you do not want to do the will of God, it cannot help you. The particular point in this discussion is that the law's function is to show what is right and what is wrong. The results are that when you know the law and then do wrong, you feel worse than when you had not known your sin and you are more responsible for your actions.

Chapter 28

MAN IS HOPELESS BECAUSE OF SIN

(Romans 7:14-21)

Do you realize that wishing you were good and that you would do good are of no real help to you?

> For I know that in me (that is, in my flesh,) dwelleth no good thing (Rom. 7:18).

When we look at Romans 7:14-21 we see that there is no chance to be free from sin as long as we live in the flesh. You and I can cherish in our hearts and minds the happy assurance that deliverance has been effected. Later we will study what Paul says about it, but here he is showing how impossible it is to escape from the blight of sin in our own strength. Paul begins by stating, "For we know that the law is spiritual: but I am carnal, sold under sin" (Rom. 7:14). The words *spiritual* and *carnal* are significant as Paul uses them here. We need to understand them as he did because they refer to two different influences that can affect us.

When we speak of the "spiritual," we refer to that which comes through and by the Holy Spirit of God, from God's presence: a principle from God Himself, brought us by His Holy Spirit. The word *carnal* is a principle that emanates through the senses: what we hear, see, taste, smell, and touch. This is not to say that the one is immaterial and mental, while the other is material and physical. This distinction means that any particular conduct, no matter what it is, may be influenced from either of two sources: (1) the spiritual — the reality of the presence of God revealed to us by His Holy Spirit resulting in spiritual conduct; or (2) the carnal — the way we think or feel about things in our own selves, in which case the conduct would be carnal.

Paul writes:

> For we know that the law is spiritual: but I am carnal, sold under sin (Rom. 7:14).

In other words, we know that the law, that is, the Ten Commandments and the Scripture itself, comes from God; but I in my own ego, my own human personality, "am carnal." I was born and reared in the flesh; I am of human nature. I am "sold under sin." This phrase is perhaps even more significant than it first appears. It would seem that this refers to a form of bondage, and it could be said that I am in some kind of slavery.

> For that which I do I allow not: for what I would, that do I not; but what I hate, that do I (Rom. 7:15).

That sounds confusing — and it is. In the phrase "that which I do," the word *do* is a translation of the Greek word that means "practice." So the thought being expressed is: that which I usually practice; that which I customarily do.

When Paul says "I allow not" he means he does not approve of his own actions; "for what I would [a short way of saying what I want to do, what I really prefer to do] that do I not; but what I hate." Here the word *hate* is the opposite of the word *would.* In other words, "I do not do what I want, but what I don't want: what I hate, what I am really opposed to, that I do. That is what I practice." Again, this is the classic description of the mental frame of mind of a person who wants to do right in this world, but does not have within him the power to get it done.

See how this is further emphasized in Romans 7:16: "If then I do that which I would not, I consent unto the law that it is good." If it is so that I practice the very thing I don't want to do, I judge my own conduct so that I actually am not approving the very thing I am doing. I admit that the very thing I am doing is not what I ought to do. That shows I have reference to a different course of action. I have something else in mind — the law of God. When I have the revelation from God in mind, I am not approving what I do; I am actually showing that I accept the law of God as good, and that I believe it is right.

> Now then it is no more I that do it, but sin that dwelleth in me (Rom. 7:17).

Here is an amazing statement in which we can see that the Bible is far more charitable in its estimate of us than we can ever imagine. The Bible will show us right and wrong as in a mirror so we can see where we are at fault, but the Bible also goes deeper than appearances. It looks into the heart and recognizes what the individual really wants to do. He may not want to do wrong but that is what he is doing. The Bible reveals to him that it is no more he that is doing it but "sin that dwelleth in [him]." This is marvelous to know, because it means a person can be delivered.

> For I know that in me (that is, in my flesh,) dwelleth no good thing: for to will is present with me; but how to perform that which is good I find not (Rom. 7:18).

This is Paul's way of saying he knows perfectly well there is nothing good in him because he has lived with himself. He can see how he makes up his mind to do good but he can't get it done; he wants to do good but doesn't do it. It is obvious that sin is controlling him, that he is actually under bondage to something else. This is what frustrates him.

> For the good that I would I do not: but the evil which I would not, that I do (Rom. 7:19).

This is the pathetic confession of a good man. The good things he wants to do, he does not practice; but the evil he does not want to do and is opposed to is what he practices.

> Now if I do that I would not, it is no more I that do it, but sin that dwelleth in me (Rom. 7:20).

Paul says if he practices what he does not approve, he is not really his own boss; he is in bondage. He goes on to say,

> I find then a law, that, when I would do good, evil is present with me (Rom. 7:21).

All through this passage we have the underlying recognition that man himself is not free, that he is actually in bondage. This is actually a description of repentance as seen from within the soul. Some people would call it a subjective description of repentance because it describes how he feels on the inside. He is acknowledging that the very actions he performs are against his own desires for he is not his own boss. He cannot even do what he wants to do. Paul will lead his readers away from this condition soon. Believers are able to be completely free from all these things.

Chapter 29

SIN CAUSES CONFLICT IN A MAN

(Romans 7:22-25)

Do you know that every sincere Christian is involved in a conflict within himself which can be won only through Jesus Christ?

> But I see another law in my members, warring against the law of my mind, and bringing me into captivity to the law of sin which is in my members (Rom. 7:23).

In these words the apostle Paul describes a spiritual situation in his own experience. Here he is completing his discussion of the feelings within his own heart. This is how he feels as a person who wants to do right in the sight of God. He has identified two primary principles: spiritual and carnal. The believer is a person who is involved in an experience in which both of these principles affect him. The believer has in him the old human nature, which is subject to the things of the world; and he also has in him, by the grace of God, the new nature in Christ Jesus, which by the power of God wants to go the way of the Lord.

Paul's human nature would lead him into bondage under the law of sin in his members; but Paul delights, according to verse 22, in the law of God. Yet the frustration he experienced continually made him miserable. He felt as though he were chained to his own sinful nature and could not get rid of it. He rejoiced in the gospel, in the promises of God; but his lament in verse 23 indicates the terrible warfare within him: "O wretched man that I am! who shall deliver me from the body of this death?" (Rom. 7:24).

This dilemma with which Paul was faced was much like a man trying to get free from his shadow. It cannot be done; no matter where one goes, his shadow will be with him. No one can escape dealing with himself, and this was Paul's problem. The panorama in verses 23 and 24 is an overall picture of the helpless spiritual condition of all who put their trust in Jesus Christ while still living in their human bodies. There is a sense in which this is a spiritual tragedy. The believer wants to do what is pleasing in God's sight, but all the time there is something pulling the other way. In the following studies we will find that believers can get completely free, but not if they face this in their own strength.

When Paul writes, "O wretched man that I am! who shall deliver me from the body of this death?" some say that the language implies Paul thinks of himself as if he is experiencing the offensive practice sometimes carried out by the Romans toward their criminals: If a man was found guilty of a vicious crime, they would chain him to a dead body that was decaying steadily and leave him bound up with it. This is apparently the way Paul feels about his own flesh. His own human nature was sinful in spite of everything he has tried to do; it held him down, and he felt as though he were chained to it. "The body of this death" — this dead body, this human nature of his — caused him to cry, "O wretched man that I am!"

Truly Christ is the answer. In verse 25 we read, "I thank God through Jesus Christ our Lord." We could stop here for a long time. When we reach this spot we want to rest on it. It is as if we had been walking in a swamp, and finally came to a rock we could put our feet on. This is where Paul has finally arrived, and he thanks God that deliverance will come through Jesus Christ. Since that is the case, "So then with the mind I myself serve the law of God." He expects God to deliver him, and he looks forward to this. ". . . but with the flesh the law of sin" (Rom. 7:25). This would seem to indicate that as long as Paul lives, as long as he is in the flesh, his tendency to be selfish and proud is as natural as breathing; but, thank God, his deliverance is coming. When he counts his body dead, he will be free; but as long as he allows it to live, it will not let him be free.

Verses 14-25 describe what it would be like for a man who is good to be afflicted by a consciousness of the sin that is in him; but we can be grateful he is not defeated. Our salvation was secured for us by none other than the living Lord Jesus Christ. Let me suggest something of real interest: in these verses of chapter 7 the pronoun *I* is repeated many times, but as we approach a study of chapter 8 you will notice there is no *I* in it. Instead we will find a new word, *Spirit*. A comparison brings profound insight: as long as one is limited to self, "I," there will be trouble; but there is victory and deliverance through the "Spirit."

Chapter 30

DELIVERANCE IS EFFECTED BY THE SPIRIT

(Romans 8:1-2)

Do you realize there is no doubt as to the total deliverance of every believer in and through the Lord Jesus Christ?

> For the law of the Spirit of life in Christ Jesus hath made me free from the law of sin and death (Rom. 8:2).

The apostle Paul is interested in showing the believers at Rome more and more the meaning of the gospel for them so they may enter into it more fully. In chapters 6 and 7 and now in chapter 8 he discusses the fact that sin is a very real part of living and there is only one way to be delivered from sin. We must count ourselves dead in our human nature so we may be raised from the dead by the Spirit of God.

Paul has been anxious in this letter to make sure that everyone sees himself as guilty before God. Because sin threatens with bondage, it can only be escaped by death — one must die in the Lord Jesus Christ to also be raised with Him. Here in chapter 8 Paul shows us that the grace of Jesus Christ, activated within us by the Holy Spirit, is greater than all our sins.

> There is therefore now no condemnation to them which are in Christ Jesus, who walk not after the flesh, but after the Spirit (Rom. 8:1).

There will be no calling into court, no judgment, for the person who is in Christ Jesus:

> For the law of the Spirit of life in Christ Jesus hath made me free from the law of sin and death (Rom. 8:2).

The word *law* here means the inward uniformity, the natural way of doing, of the Spirit of life which has made us free from the natural way of sin and death.

This can be illustrated by comparing two elements in the natural world that are opposed to each other: water and fire. Think for a moment about them. Water always seeks the lowest possible level; it runs downhill. Fire always tries to get as high as it can; it shoots straight up. Note, also, that water will extinguish fire, and fire will evaporate water. You cannot have fire and water in the same place.

That is the way it is with the flesh and the Spirit: you cannot have them both in the same place. The flesh, like water, goes down; the Spirit, like fire, goes up. Yet here is an interesting fact. If you put water in a kettle, the water will go to the bottom of the kettle. But if you put the kettle over fire, the power of the fire will go through the kettle into the water; then the water rises like fire. Of course, it goes up in steam, but it acts just like fire. Why? Because the power of the fire (the heat) is in it. If that vapor or mist gets too far away from the fire and its heat, it will condense into little drops of water and fall to the ground. It will act as water did before.

This helps us understand some people who have become believers. There have been cases where people have accepted Christ and for a length of time have walked with Him. Their lives have been so changed and they were happy and joyful. Sadly, some people have stopped walking with the Lord; they no longer read their Bibles or pray. They have no joy in the Lord and they begin to act exactly as they did before they accepted Christ. You might say, "It did not do them any good." But let us put it like this: as long as the fire was operative, as long as the power of the fire was there, the water was lifted up and carried along by the heat that was in it. When it got too far away from the fire, the heat dissipated, and then when the vapor cooled off it returned to its former state and fell down.

This is what often happens to believers. Remember, when we are born again, when we are regenerated and become believers, it does not mean we become angels or that our nature is changed. Some of us are extremely aware of this. Sometimes it is shocking to learn how much we can think and act as we used to think and act. If we are close to the Lord, the Holy Spirit will be like fire in us, and the heat of the fire will lift us up and make us act as if we were fire. As long as the power of the Holy Spirit is within us, we will act spiritual.

If you hold a pencil up over a table and then let go of it, what does the pencil do? It falls down. The pencil does not have any strength of itself. Suppose you don't let go of it. Why doesn't it fall? Because you are holding it. How long will it stay there? As long as you hold it. Under what conditions will it rise? If you lift it. Under what conditions will that pencil move to the right? If you move your hand. This is similar to our lives as Christians. When we trust in the Lord, He holds us up and moves us. This is what it means to be saved by the power of God. We are actually being affected by the power of God — He lifts us and carries us His way. This is the law of the Spirit of life in Christ Jesus. The power of His hand has set us free from the law of sin and death just as your hand freed the pencil from the law of gravity so it did what you wanted it to do. This is how the life in Christ is lived.

Chapter 31

THE CARNAL MIND

(Romans 8:3-8)

Did you know that no child of God is ever free to act as a human being?

> So then they that are in the flesh cannot please God (Rom. 8:8).

Does that sound strange to you? Perhaps an illustration will help explain. If I were to say that no married woman is ever free to act as a single woman, I am sure you would know exactly what is meant by that. It is like saying no man who is in the Marines is free to act as if he is a civilian. The same truth is involved in being a child of God. When the believer is born again he becomes related to Christ, and he then has two levels of conduct: the first is commonly called the "natural," which centers in self; and the second is called the "spiritual," which centers in Christ.

Paul says that all we have from other human beings — starting with parents, home, school, community, church, nation, and culture — would be called flesh. All that we have from God directly through fellowship with Him would be called Spirit. Every believer is involved in the flesh because he is born of human parents, lives with human beings, and speaks human language. So he has the flesh, yet because he is born again and is from God, he has the Spirit. This means he has to deal with the flesh and also with the Spirit; he deals with mankind and he deals with God. The problem that arises is: Which one of these two shall predominate?

Most commonly man will walk after the flesh. He will make his own choices and plan his own program according to what he is interested in as a human being. Paul calls that being carnal. This does not mean something vicious, but earthly. On the other hand it is spiritual for a person to be inwardly influenced by the Spirit of God through the Lord Jesus Christ; and this Paul calls spiritual.

> That the righteousness of the law might be fulfilled in us, who walk not after the flesh, but after the Spirit (Rom. 8:4).

These are individuals who walk not according to human interests and ideas, but according to the presence of God by the Spirit.

Paul states that the righteousness of the law can be fulfilled in believers who walk after the Spirit. The righteousness of the law would be the righteousness within those who do the right thing because of the consequences, because they want right to happen. We will see later how this righteousness of the law can be fulfilled in the believer. In this verse let us think of the word *fulfilled* in the sense of the believer's being filled to overflowing. The believer normally does more than the law requires.

The law says, with reference to property, "Thou shalt not steal." This means that you have what is yours and the other fellow has what is his, and each should keep his own. You will recognize that this is not enough for a child of God. He doesn't say, "What is mine is mine, and I will keep it"; nor does he say foolishly, "All that is mine I will give to someone else." Actually he exercises a stewardship over what he has. As a need arises, he will give to those in need, which is far more than not stealing. He does not take away from others—he actually gives to them.

The law says, "Thou shalt not bear false witness." Very simply, this means "Thou shalt not lie." Now it is one thing not to tell a lie, but a child of God is not satisfied with that. He goes beyond that: he wants to tell the truth. The same is true with reference to "Thou shalt not kill." The believer does not really satisfy the Spirit within him if he simply makes it a point not to kill people: the believer will undertake to save. The child of God goes beyond the requirements of the law and thus fulfills the righteousness of the law as he walks according to the Spirit.

> For they that are after the flesh do mind the things of the flesh; but they that are after the Spirit the things of the Spirit (Rom. 8:5).

Paul would say that those interested solely in human things

are in the flesh, but those who want to do what is pleasing in God's sight are in the Spirit.

> For to be carnally minded is death; but to be spiritually minded is life and peace (Rom. 8:6).

A person who lives only to please himself will end up in a spiritual condition that is spoken of as "death": dead in trespasses and sin. But those who are conscious of doing what is pleasing to God will find this leads to life and peace. The intrinsic nature of man is not that of obedience.

> Because the carnal mind is enmity against God: for it is not subject to the law of God, neither indeed can be (Rom. 8:7).

The mind that is centered in self is not like God, because if it were like God it would be centered in Christ. The person who is centered in self is actually hostile to the things of God.

> So then they that are in the flesh cannot please God (Rom. 8:8).

This is the simple truth about all of human life. The natural human being as such cannot please God because he is interested only in self. If you are a person who has not thought about these things you may be inclined to doubt these words; but I urge you to read them carefully and think them through, because if you intend to follow the Lord Jesus Christ, the first thing you must do is deny yourself, take up the cross, and follow Him.

Chapter 32

IN THE SPIRIT

(Romans 8:9-14)

Did you know that no believer is ever left to himself?

> For as many as are led by the Spirit of God, they are the sons of God (Rom. 8:14).

It is natural for us to hold a man responsible for his conduct. When we see what a man does and think about his actions, we are disposed either to praise him for doing good or to blame him for doing wrong. It is true that the whole process of salvation can be seen in the field of conduct. "By their fruits ye shall know them." A person who is saved will be godly in his conduct. The fact that those who are outside of Christ are "lost" will show up in their unrighteous conduct. This would be simple enough in general, and we would be inclined to think that whoever does everything he should do is godly, while the person who does the things he should not do is ungodly.

This issue was confused in New Testament times because of the Jews. They had the law, which described how righteousness should be apparent, so they knew what God required of them. What complicated the situation was that they tried to achieve this righteousness by themselves. Paul pointed out in the Epistle to the Romans that no one is righteous. No one is in himself good enough or strong enough to do all the things God wants him to do. Everyone needs to be saved. Paul reiterated that this salvation is free and complete, and it is available through Jesus Christ.

In Romans 8 Paul shows how this plan of salvation provides for a difference in conduct. New conduct is produced by the Holy Spirit's living and working in believers, activating the will of Christ in them. The Bible tells us that only one person ever lived who kept the law of God perfectly: Jesus of Nazareth, who was the Christ, the Son of the living God. The Bible also affirms that in the plan of salvation believers can be in Christ, and He will be in them, inclining them to do the will of God. This is activated in the believer by the Holy Spirit of God, given to believers to bring into their consciousness the things of Christ. As the Holy Spirit shows the things of Christ to the human heart, He will activate the obedient will of Christ in the human heart of each person who believes.

> But ye are not in the flesh, but in the Spirit, if so be that the Spirit of God dwell in you (Rom. 8:9).

Paul has been talking about the flesh and the Spirit. The word *flesh* covers everything human, and the word *Spirit* covers everything that is from God. This does not mean that everything in the flesh is equally evil; but it is of the flesh in that it consists of mere human ideas and effort. Paul says believers are not in the flesh "but in the Spirit, if so be that the Spirit of God dwell in you." He reinforces this by saying, "Now if any man have not the Spirit of Christ, he is none of his."

Having the Spirit of Christ within is essential for believers. We should remind ourselves that not everyone has the Spirit of Christ in him. This is where Paul points out that while salvation is offered to all, not all men will accept it. The simple truth is that if the Spirit of God is not dwelling in us, we are not His. In the tenth verse we find that the Spirit-filled man has the two natures: "And if Christ be in you, the body is dead because of sin; but the Spirit is life because of righteousness" (Rom. 8:10). He has his human body, which is dead because of sin, but the Spirit he received from Christ is life because of righteousness, and it moves him into doing the will of God, which is life. Since he possesses both natures something must happen.

> But if the Spirit of him that raised up Jesus from the dead dwell in you, he that raised up Christ from the dead shall also quicken your mortal bodies by his Spirit that dwelleth in you (Rom. 8:11).

Therefore, the believer's consciousness, his state of mind, is that of being resurrected from the dead. There is in him the newness of life — action can now follow the spiritual, because the carnal is reckoned to be dead. He will be lifted from the sinful into the spiritual, into being one of God's own.

> Therefore, brethren, we are debtors, not to the flesh, to live after the flesh (Rom. 8:12).

Believers are under no obligation to respond to the flesh anymore. They do not have to do the wrong thing. They do not have to be selfish. They can be free.

> For if ye live after the flesh, ye shall die: but if ye through the Spirit do mortify the deeds of the body, ye shall live (Rom. 8:13).

Apparently believers do have a choice in what they accept. They have the flesh in them and they have the Holy Spirit in them, so they can turn one way or the other; if they go their own way they will be in the flesh, and if they do the things of the Lord, they will be in the Spirit, and they will have victory.

> For as many as are led by the Spirit of God, they are the sons of God (Rom. 8:14).

There need be no doubt as to the significance of the operation of the Holy Spirit within the child of God.

Since the Holy Spirit is working in believers, they belong to God. If the Holy Spirit is not working in a person, he does not belong to God. The first indication that the Holy Spirit is working in a person is that he will trust God. He will turn to God, yielding to Him and opening his heart to receive His blessing — then he belongs to God. If a person is not inclined to believe, to yield to God, and to open his heart to Christ, then he does not belong because the evidence is not there.

"For as many as are led by the Spirit of God, they are the sons of God."

Chapter 33

CHILDREN OF GOD

(Romans 8:15-18)

Do you realize that every believer is an adopted child of God?

> And if children, then heirs; heirs of God, and joint-heirs with Christ; if so be that we suffer with him, that we may be also glorified together (Rom. 8:17).

One of the most profound truths the Bible has revealed is that whereas on the one hand whosoever will may come, on the other hand it is also true that whosoever will not does not come, and whosoever believeth not is condemned already. Many seem to want to hear the call of God for them, even though they treat the gospel with indifference. They want to be sure they are invited. They will resent it, and often are offended and moved into open controversy and argument, if one brings out the other aspect of the truth which simply says, "He that hath the Son hath life; and he that hath not the Son of God hath not life" (1 John 5:12). Some do not want to hear this; they want to hear that everything is done for them but nothing is done against them. They have nothing to expect but disappointment.

Why do some individuals want to receive the invitation even if they do not intend to come, despite the fact that they seem indifferent? Perhaps it is so that in case they change their minds, they can turn to it. But there is a statement in the Bible that occurs several times, and sometimes I think we do not hear it spoken nearly enough: "God is not mocked." What that really means is that no one can make a fool out of God. Remember the story of the ten virgins — five of whom were wise and five foolish? We should not miss the last part of the story which tells about the foolish virgins coming to the door and finding it closed. God is gracious and merciful and slow to anger and plenteous in mercy, but He can be provoked. He has anger toward the wicked.

We have noted clearly that believers are children of God, but not in a natural way, as if by being human they are children of God. No, they are adopted as children of God.

> For ye have not received the spirit of bondage again to fear; but ye have received the Spirit of adoption, whereby we cry, Abba, Father (Rom. 8:15).

Believers have received the Spirit that adopts them into the family of God. There is one trait all believers possess: everyone who is a genuine believer in the Lord Jesus Christ has the happy assurance he does belong to God. This is basic. It is not based on any favorable estimate of himself but is the consciousness that Christ Jesus offered Himself for him. The believer is received in Him. Then the Holy Spirit of God takes the mind of Christ and activates it in the believer. Then just as the Lord Jesus looking up to His Father would call Him "Father," so also the believer finds himself moved from within to look up to God and call Him "Father." That is the meaning of "Abba." God is our Father because He has begotten us by His Word. The word *Abba* means more than "Father"; it is what we call a diminutive. Tommy is the diminutive of Tom, daddy is the diminutive of dad. "Abba" is like "Daddy" — it is what a child would say on his father's knee.

The believer can have all this in his heart about almighty God: he can look up into His face and call Him Father because he belongs to Him; he has in him the Holy Spirit of God who has adopted him into God's family.

> The Spirit itself beareth witness with our spirit, that we are the children of God (Rom. 8:16).

This is how the believer will know. Some years ago when I read about John Calvin, I was extremely interested in what Calvin said when asked how he knew the Bible was for him. He said he knew that the Bible was for him in the same way he knew the face he saw in the mirror was his own face. If a person looks into the Bible he will know it is for him; therefore, when a believer looks up into the face of God, if he has the Holy Spirit in his heart, he will know that God belongs to him. The Holy

Spirit will bear witness with his spirit that he is a child of God.

> And if children, then heirs; heirs of God, and joint-heirs with Christ; if so be that we suffer with him, that we may be also glorified together (Rom. 8:17).

In the first marvelous statement of this passage it was affirmed that since the believer is a child, then he is an heir, and he inherits God. He is a joint-heir with Christ and inherits everything He gives. The second part of the verse protects anyone from foolishly making this so broad as to include everyone. Lest anyone imagine this is for all mankind Paul adds the explanation, "if so be that we suffer with him, that we may be also glorified together."

I think this suffering with Christ refers primarily to the fact that we suffer unto death; we die with Him as He died on Calvary's cross. In Romans 6 it was written that believers are to be buried with Him by baptism into His death, that they might be raised again in the newness of life. They are planted with Him in the likeness of His death that they might be raised in the likeness of His resurrection. And if they die to self with Christ, they will also be glorified together. They will be made fruitful by the indwelling Holy Spirit of God. Who will be heirs? Everyone who suffers with Christ.

> For I reckon that the sufferings of this present time are not worthy to be compared with the glory which shall be revealed in us (Rom. 8:18).

The suffering of this present time is denying self, always yielding to God. And Paul says the sufferings of this present time are not worthy to be compared with the glory which shall be revealed. This is the prospect believers have in Him.

Chapter 34

HELPED BY THE SPIRIT

(Romans 8:19-27)

Do you understand that the "Spirit also helpeth our infirmities"?

In our last study we noted that the power of the Holy Spirit works on the natural elements in the believer to resurrect these natural elements from the condition of death in sin. The Holy Spirit gives them a responsiveness to God so each believer has a consciousness that he now belongs to God, being led and lifted by the Spirit of God.

We shall now see that Paul projects this truth into all of the affairs of believers. On every side in every way that which is natural is limited in itself to suffering in this world, but the outlook in salvation is hopeful because of the power of God. Paul seems to imply that God's purpose in creating the world was for the use of His people throughout the ages. In other words, it is as though God created the world in the natural, knowing that it would need to be taken over by the spiritual to be made eternal and to be made useful for the whole purpose of God.

This is not an easy portion of Scripture to understand. The reader may often feel he is walking through underbrush. He cannot even see a step ahead as he goes through it. I think we can gain understanding more readily if we use the word creation throughout rather than the word *creature*. Thus we would read, "For the earnest expectation of the *creation* waiteth for the manifestation of the sons of God." The sons of God will be manifested when, in Christ Jesus, they are shown as being delivered from the bondage of the flesh and lifted into the freedom of the spiritual. This is like the manifestation of Jesus Christ in this world, as He was shown in authority over the natural processes. Something similar is apparently intimated for those who are in Him.

> For the creature was made subject to vanity, not willingly, but by reason of him who hath subjected the same in hope, because the creature itself also shall be delivered from the bondage of corruption into the glorious liberty of the children of God (Rom. 8:20,21).

Paul tells us here that creation was made subject to the emptiness of man's mind, the sinfulness of man's way of doing things, "not willingly," not because this was a good thing or even the purpose of it, but because God did this in the expectation that creation would be redeemed through the Lord Jesus Christ. ". . . because the *creation* itself also shall be delivered from the bondage of corruption into the glorious liberty of the children of God."

The bondage of corruption would be the death that comes upon the whole creation, marked by the sentence of death. Everything in the natural world deteriorates into death, yet in the resurrection of Jesus Christ this process is reversed. The children of God are to be raised in Him, and there is a sense in which the liberty of the children of God from this sentence is into glory. It is in that sense it is called "the glorious liberty."

> For we know that the whole creation groaneth and travaileth in pain together until now. And not only they, but ourselves also, which have the first fruits of the Spirit, even we ourselves groan within ourselves, waiting for the adoption, to wit, the redemption of our body (Rom. 8:22,23).

There is much suffering in the world because of the many limitations upon the natural world. And not only all created things, but believers also, who are already united with the Lord Jesus Christ, are awaiting adoption and redemption.

Paul goes on to reveal that one of these days we shall be lifted our of our bodily limitations to time and space, and out of our limitations in understanding.

> For we are saved by hope: but hope that is seen is not hope: for what a man seeth, why doth he yet hope for? But if we hope for that we see not, then do we with patience wait for it (Rom. 8:24,25).

My understanding of these verses is that by the grace of God believers are enabled to look forward to something better than anything they have here. His promises are greater than any of the natural processes, which will be overcome in the power of God, first seen in the resurrection of Jesus Christ, and which will be seen again in the resurrection and the fulfillment of the children of God.

> Likewise the Spirit also helpeth our infirmities: for we know not what we should pray for as we ought: but the Spirit itself maketh intercession for us with groanings which cannot be uttered. And he that searcheth the hearts knoweth what is the mind of the Spirit, because he maketh intercession for the saints according to the will of God (Rom. 8:26,27).

Here again we have the Spirit of God, the power of God, being exercised on our behalf in the natural and bringing us out of it. We are not limited even to our best intentions as Christians because we are lifted above that.

In these verses we have Paul's statement of confident expectation that believers are being helped constantly by the Holy Spirit of God. God is working on our behalf to set us free from and lift us above our human limitations, even in our minds and thoughts as believing people. This is intended to give us strong confidence and trust in God. He will take care of us.

Chapter 35

TOTAL CONFIDENCE

(Romans 8:28)

Do you think it is wise for a Christian to have no uneasiness about anything?

> And we know that all things work together for good to them that love God, to them who are the called according to his purpose (Rom. 8:28).

This is one of the most wonderful verses in the Bible. It is always at the top of the list of precious promises in Scripture, yet it is one of the easiest statements in the Bible to misunderstand. In verse 27 it is written: "[the Holy Spirit] maketh intercession for the saints according to the will of God." We know that God is over all and in all. God deals with all men, with believers and with nonbelievers. His dealing is in righteousness and goodness. While it is true that God is gracious, kind, merciful, and benevolent to everyone, it is also true that He is a rewarder of those who diligently seek Him. That does not mean He plays favorites; but it does mean He will deal with His own in special benevolence because they have willingly drawn close to Him.

However, if anyone does not diligently seek God he will not get that particular benefit from Him. The Holy Spirit is not a respecter of persons; He will make intercession for anyone who believes in Jesus Christ. It is not that God is unfair, nor is He only interested in those who believe. Christ's death has the promise of grace to any who believe in Him, which those who do not believe in Him cannot have; and it is for this reason we know that "all things work together for good to them that love God."

When we say that all things work together for good to them that love God, there is at this point much loose interpretation and shallow application. Many remember just a part, ". . . all things work together for good," and place a period there. We need to read the entire verse. When it says that "all things work together for good to them that love God," the point is that when they love God they are in line for more blessing. The gospel promises are not intended to say that everything will turn out fine regardless; that is not true. This is a special statement, and it has a particular bearing on the ministry of the Holy Spirit in the experience of the believer. The statement makes it obvious that the overruling providence of God is exercised on behalf of those who seek Him and His glory. This is not on behalf of them as opposed to someone else; it is not that God is blessing Tom because He will not bless Dick or Harry. God is blessing Tom because he believes; He would bless Dick if he believed.

We recognize that God is willing to share His grace with all men. It is still true that not all men believe in God nor do they accept Jesus Christ, and people who do not accept Jesus Christ do not have this blessing. Isn't that fair to everyone? It does not mean that believers are blessed at the expense of others; believers are blessed beyond others, and there is a reason. They have responded beyond others, and they have reached for more of the blessing of God.

We could ask ourselves this: Are there any people for whom things do not work out? Yes, of course. There are any number of individuals in this world whose experiences are tragic; and when they suffer they never receive any benefit from it — they suffer in vain.

Who are these people? They are those who try to make out by themselves without turning to God. For them there is no promise that things will turn out better; they will reap what they sow. For many people, reaping what they sow will place them in serious trouble. But for those who put their trust in the Lord (which means they deny themselves and reckon themselves dead) there is no point in carrying out the wrongs they planned in the past, because the body is dead.

Believers will receive from God blessing that the Lord Jesus Christ actually earned and which He already received. They are heirs of God, joint heirs with Christ Jesus. When a woman marries, she shares her husband's estate; and when believers are married to Jesus Christ they share His benefits, His property. They have much more than they had before. This does not do others any harm; but those who have come closer to God receive more blessing. Other people could come closer to God if they would. We should all understand this when we read that "all thing work together for good to them that love God, to them who are called according to his purpose."

If people are following their own desires they will suffer in vain; whereas all who deny self and yield to Christ will find everything that happens to them beneficial. This is the meaning of the promise and we know that the Holy Spirit is making intercession for us. If we believe in Christ and put our trust in Him, when suffering comes it will not be so bad because we have reckoned ourselves dead. The fact that we trust in Him means that God can make this experience become something beneficial.

Chapter 36

SAVED IN HIS LOVE

(Romans 8:29-39)

If a man accepts Christ do you think there is any chance he will ever be lost?

> For I am persuaded, that neither death, nor life, nor angels, nor principalities, nor powers, nor things present, nor things to come, nor height, nor depth, nor any other creature, shall be able to separate us from the love of God, which is in Christ Jesus our Lord (Rom. 8:38,39).

These are the words with which the apostle Paul concludes the eighth chapter of Romans. In Romans 8:29-39 we see how Paul argues for the confidence we noticed in our last study. He sets forth the basis of his total confidence, starting with five tremendous statements that represent things God does. This is what he says:

> For whom he did foreknow, he also did predestinate to be conformed to the image of his Son, that he might be the first-born among many brethren. Moreover whom he did predestinate, them he also called: and whom he called, them he also justified: and whom he justified, them he also glorified (Rom. 8:29,30).

With regard to the word *predestinate*, the following should be pointed out. Notice that "he also did predestinate to be conformed to the image of his Son." Whenever you think of the word *predestinate*, place your emphasis on the latter part of the word, *destinate*. What is a person's destination? It is his ultimate end. The *pre* means only that where this will be is known beforehand. Where is his destination? He is "predestinated to be conformed to the image of his Son."

In other words, God has in mind that every believer in the Lord Jesus Christ will be made in His likeness, and in the future our destination is to be like Him in the very presence of God. That is already known. Let me emphasize that in the Bible the word *predestination* is never used of sinners. The Bible does not say that God predestinates anyone to be lost. The word is used only with believers and has to do with their being in heaven with the Lord.

In a sense we have here a sketch of almost the entire gospel of salvation. Every part of salvation is embodied in these five verbs: *foreknow, predestinate, calls, justifies, glorifies*. Some people believe that the way these five verbs are listed should be studied in order as they occur one after the other in chronological fashion: first, God foreknows; then He predestinates, then He calls, then He justifies, and finally He glorifies. Others understand this to mean that these five things are done at once in the grace of God and are the five aspects of God's grace, much like five petals on a rose. They would claim we can't very well say one is first and another is second; undoubtedly they are related to each other, but all come from the center. There are people who think these five things are simultaneous insofar as the grace of God in Christ Jesus is concerned. In any case, they are tremendous, because they indicate that it is God who saves us and our salvation depends upon Him.

In verse 31 Paul argues for confidence in moving on in Christian living. This argument is grounded in the grace of God.

> What shall we then say to these things? If God be for us, who can be against us? (Rom. 8:31).

After all, if God is the one who foreknows and predestinates believers, who calls, justifies, and glorifies believers, what then can anyone say? These things are overwhelming. Certainly we should be confident that all things work together for good to a person who is receiving the grace of God in such glorious fashion.

Paul also argues for confidence that is grounded on the sacrifice of Christ on Calvary.

> He that spared not his own Son, but delivered him up for us all, how shall he not with him also freely give us all things? (Rom. 8:32).

If God would send Jesus Christ to die for us, do you think He would hold anything back? We can be sure God will do anything on behalf of believers. It will be quite proper for us to be confident that all things will work together for our good.

This confidence is grounded also in God's action in justifying us.

> Who shall lay any thing to the charge of God's elect? It is God that justifieth (Rom. 8:33).

This could be asked in the form of a question and read thus, "Who shall lay anything to the charge of God's elect? God that justifieth? He is the One who makes us right; do you think He will hold anything against us?" This argument for confidence is grounded also in Christ's present intercession:

> Who is he that condemneth? It is Christ that died, yea rather, that is risen again, who is even at the right hand of God, who also maketh intercession for us (Rom. 8:34).

Paul is saying in effect: Do you think that Christ Jesus, who is right now praying for us, will condemn us? Paul argues that this doesn't make sense. God would not condemn us, nor would Christ, and no one else has the authority to do it. Paul is establishing a basis for complete confidence in the goodness and mercy of God.

Paul then surveys all the different things he feels could be against believers:

> Who shall separate us from the love of Christ? shall tribulation, or distress, or persecution, or famine, or nakedness, or peril, or sword? As it is written, For thy sake we are killed all the day long; we are accounted as sheep for the slaughter. Nay, in all these things we are more than conquerors through him that loved us (Rom. 8:35-37).

God's love is able to overcome every unfavorable element, factor, or condition. Almighty God is on the believer's side, and He intends to help us.

Chapter 37

THE CHILDREN OF THE PROMISE

(Romans 9:1-8)

Do you think if a person is born into a home of believing parents, he would naturally be a believer?

> They which are the children of the flesh, these are not the children of God: but the children of the promise are counted for the seed (Rom. 9:8).

There is much confusion about what is meant by the word *believer*. Just who is a believer? We know that some are believers while others are not. What is it that makes a person a believer? In Paul's time there were many who claimed to belong to God who actually did not. One of these groups was a special burden to Paul, because they were his own kinsmen, Jews.

> I say the truth in Christ, I lie not, my conscience also bearing me witness in the Holy Ghost, that I have great heaviness and continual sorrow in my heart. For I could wish that myself were accursed from Christ for my brethren, my kinsmen according to the flesh: who are Israelites; to whom pertaineth the adoption, and the glory, and the covenants, and the giving of the law, and the service of God, and the promises; whose are the fathers, and of whom as concerning the flesh Christ came, who is over all, God blessed for ever (Rom. 9:1-5).

Here Paul claims to have a day-by-day burden, wanting his kinsmen, the Jews, to belong to Christ. They were among the people who were called to belong to God and receive His blessing, and those to whom God would reveal Himself. He had given them the Ten Commandments, the promises of the law, and a temple in which to worship. Many of their forefathers had believed in God, and furthermore Christ Himself was a Jew. Yet in spite of the fact that the Jews had all these blessings, their faces were turned away from God.

> Not as though the word of God hath taken none effect. For they are not all Israel, which are of Israel: neither, because they are the seed of Abraham, are they all children: but, In Isaac shall thy seed be called (Rom. 9:6,7).

There were some Jews who did believe, and Paul was one of them. "For they are not all Israel which are of Israel." This is an extremely important statement. All of the children born in Israel do not count as Israelites. Even though they are the seed of Abraham and are descendants of his biologically, this does not make them the children of God in the sense of the covenant; they do not really belong to Him. Remember Abraham had two sons: Ishmael was of the flesh and Isaac was of promise. Ishmael did not receive the blessing but Isaac did. Paul is pointing out that not all in the group who are flesh descendants of Abraham will be saved.

Paul then goes on to say:

> That is, They which are the children of the flesh, these are not the children of God: but the children of the promise are counted for the seed (Rom. 9:8).

Those who believe in the promises of God are the ones who really belong. We should pause and think how important this truth is for us. When a person grows up in a believing home and has taken part in the work of the church, it is a great temptation to consider him a believer. But has that person received the Lord Jesus Christ? Does he trust in the promises of God? The fact that he was born into a believing home gave him an advantage but he could still be lost.

That is the way it was with Israel, and Paul was concerned about those people. He had great heaviness and continual sorrow in his heart because of them. We are sometimes inclined to be almost casual about those who are not born-again believers, but this was not true of Paul. We, too, should be very much concerned. A young student told me that one time he was talking with an elderly man who had gone to church regularly all of his life and who now needed help. The student felt the man did not really trust God for his salvation, and he asked the man if he thought he would go to heaven when he died. The man said he thought he would and began to recount all the good things he had done: he had gone to church regularly, been decent to his family, paid his debts, and tried to be a good neighbor. The young man then said to him, "You are depending on yourself to get there"; and when the old man asked what he should do, the young man said, "If you trust in God you will know for sure you are going to heaven because Christ Jesus died for you, and God will save you if you trust in Him because of that."

Chapter 38

THE PURPOSE OF GOD

(Romans 9:9-18)

Do you think it is unfair that God should save some people and not others?

The truth of God I want to consider now is that not everyone will be saved. In the Sermon on the Mount, Jesus told us "not every house will stand the test": houses built on the rock will stand; those not built on the rock will collapse. In the same passage Jesus said that not everyone who calls on the name of God will be saved, but only those who do His will. Regardless of how it seems, so far as the human mind is concerned, not everyone will be saved.

We are reminded again of the story of the ten virgins. There is nothing in the story that indicates the five foolish virgins ever did get in. In the parable of the talents the servant who had the one talent and buried it in the ground was cast out — his master took away from him what he had and cast him out with the enemies of God. In the parable of the sheep and the goats, the sheep were received into the kingdom of almighty God, while the goats were turned away.

Not even everyone who thinks he will be saved shall be saved. If anyone is uneasy about that, let me add that we do not pass judgment on ourselves: God passes judgment on us. How can we be sure we are saved? We can put our trust in the Lord Jesus Christ and be sure, not because we are good but because He is good. Paul discusses this in Romans 9. Many earnest people get the impression that because God is responsible for those who believe, that makes Him responsible for those who do not believe. Let me humbly say this: I do not think that is what the Bible teaches. If fifty men were shipwrecked on an island and a rescue ship offered to take all of them to the mainland, but only thirty accepted the invitation, was the ship to blame that the others did not accept the offer? So it is with reference to the gospel. God is not willing that any should perish but that all should come to everlasting life. But some are not willing to come.

> And not only this; but when Rebecca also had conceived by one, even by our father Isaac; (for the children being not yet born, neither having done any good or evil, that the purpose of God according to election might stand, not of works, but of him that calleth;) it was said unto her, The elder shall serve the younger. As it is written, Jacob have I loved, but Esau have I hated (Rom. 9:10-13).

It is common for people to think that this makes God responsible because it seems He chose Jacob and did not choose Esau. However, we must remember that God foreknew what these men would do. The election of God is a mystery, but God is righteous. We are told in 1 Peter: "elect according to the foreknowledge of God" (1:2).

Before the children were born God predicted that Jacob would be blessed. Was this arbitrary? Again, we must remember that although they had not yet been born nor had they done anything, God knows all things. He knew that Jacob would respond to the will of God, and He knew that Esau would sell his birthright for a mess of pottage. Jacob, the man who will seek the blessing of God, is one He will love; Esau, the man who will sell his blessing for fleshly benefits, is one whom God hates.

The phrase "the purpose of God according to election" brings us to a difficult problem of interpretation. We should be careful not to make the word *election* to read *selection*. When Paul used the word *election*, he was not thinking of the democratic political process of election; rather, he was thinking of what the word itself means, "called out." The word *election* may well refer to that operation of God wherein He will receive as His own those who respond to His call. He calls, and those who respond are the elect. Jacob would respond to the call, making him one of the elect; Esau would not respond to the call, thus he is not one of the elect.*

> What shall we say then? Is there unrighteousness with God? God forbid. For he saith to Moses, I will have mercy on whom I

> will have mercy, and I will have compassion on whom I will have compassion (Rom. 9:14,15).

On whom does God have mercy and compassion? Is it not on those who respond to Him?

> So then it is not of him that willeth, nor of him that runneth, but of God that showeth mercy (Rom. 9:16).

It is not outward performance or overt action in the world that causes a person to be saved. God will show mercy to those who call upon Him.

> For the scripture saith unto Pharaoh, Even for this same purpose have I raised thee up, that I might show my power in thee, and that my name might be declared throughout all the earth (Rom. 9:17).

God knew what Pharaoh would do but He let Pharaoh go on to show what He would do with that kind of person.

> Therefore hath he mercy on whom he will have mercy, and whom he will he hardeneth (Rom. 9:18).

Never forget that God will have mercy on those who turn to Him; He will harden and destroy those who turn away from Him. He always has and He always will.

*I have written more fully about this matter in a pamphlet, "Predestination and Election."

Chapter 39

THE SOVEREIGNTY OF GOD

(Romans 9:19-25)

Do you think people should be encouraged to think it is possible for them to understand why things happen as they do?

People often raise questions about the acts of God, and then become unhappy and tense because they do not understand why certain things happen. It is common for some to ask: If God is good, why did a particular thing happen? Or, if God is alive and cares, why doesn't He do something to stop misery? Why does He allow it? Such questions remind me of my own questions in the days of my unbelief. I can remember having such a frame of mind.

At this point in our study Paul is arguing for our full confidence in God. He raises the question: If salvation is free and available and can be had by faith, and if it is complete so that we are totally delivered from our sins and saved, then why did the Jews not have it? They struggled, and they believed in God; they were named by the name of God. Why did they not have this blessing? Paul argues that God is as He is portrayed in the gospel: gracious and benevolent. And God does provide salvation, even though the Jews missed it. Paul discusses this problem so that we might have confidence in God, even though the Jews did not accept the gospel as true.

In thinking about the Jews in this connection, we can apply these thoughts to ourselves today. Why is it that some people who call themselves believers and attend church regularly do not have peace and strength? Why do some people have joy in the Lord while others do not? Full confidence in God need not be abandoned, even though it may be threatened by the evidence that God tolerates evil, even allowing wicked men to prosper. We can learn much from Paul's approach to this problem.

> Thou wilt say then unto me, Why doth he yet find fault? For who hath resisted his will? Nay but, O man, who art thou that repliest against God? Shall the thing formed say to him that formed it, Why hast thou made me thus? Hath not the potter power over the clay, of the same lump to make one vessel unto honour, and another unto dishonour? What if God, willing to show his wrath, and to make his power known, endured with much long-suffering the vessels of wrath fitted to destruction: and that he might make known the riches of his glory on the vessels of mercy, which he had afore prepared unto glory, even us, whom he hath called, not of the Jews only, but also of the Gentiles? (Rom. 9:19-24).

Paul wants to be quite definite about this matter, and he may seem to be blunt. To the man who would ask, "Why are things as they are?" Paul would answer, "Who are you to ask?" God is answerable to no man.

Paul then points out that we need not think God unrighteous or unfair. It is not because Paul is afraid God cannot be explained, but he wants us to understand that we are not big enough to comprehend God. It is presumptuous to question God. The deeper truth Paul would emphasize here is that God is sovereign. Vanity and pride are what cause a man to feel competent to judge God.

It is always sad to see earnest, sincere people trying to explain the ways of God to persons who do not even care. People who are indifferent raise questions just for the sake of making the believer feel awkward. I met many such men when I was a young man giving my witness on the streets of Los Angeles. They were full of questions, all sharpened and ready to embarrass me. Paul would have stopped such a man in his tracks, and bluntly asked, "Who are you to ask?"

It is not man's prerogative to ask about the ways of God. It is not his privilege to judge God. Even trying to explain these things to a person will give him the wrong idea. No man has the right to ask such questions about God:

> Who art thou that repliest against God? Shall the thing formed say to him that formed it, Why hast thou made me thus? Hath not the potter power over the clay, of the same lump to make one vessel unto honour, and another unto dishonour? (Rom. 9:20, 21).

Romans 9:22-25 gives an intimation of the possible purpose of God. Paul seems to offer this by way of a help to anyone who is genuinely interested in the plan of God as revealed in His works. The idea seems to be that God may allow things to happen to show the truth in His way. "What if God, willing to show his wrath, and to make his power known," allowed Pharaoh to go on so that He might make an example of him, to show that He really is aware of how men act? Then God would show through Israel what He would do in mercy for those who obeyed Him. All of this would be a demonstration to teach. This may seem somewhat obscure, but the general lesson is plain: God will do as He sees fit. Man often fails to appreciate the wisdom of God; also he fails to recognize the purpose of God, which is to bless. What Paul would tell anyone is that man does not have the right to ask questions about the ways of God. The whole idea of attempting to judge God is evil. If a person is humble, he will bow before the will of almighty God, knowing that God made him and he is dependent upon Him.

Chapter 40

THE CHILDREN OF THE LIVING GOD

(Romans 9:26-33)

Do you think everyone is a child of God?

> And it shall come to pass, that in the place where is was said unto them, Ye are not my people; there shall they be called the children of the living God (Rom. 9:26).

Perhaps there is no other phrase more commonly used among Christians than this one: "the children of God." Actually, this is a Bible phrase. It refers to people whom God is leading to Himself. Confusion is caused by the fact that there are some today who try to make this phrase include everyone. If this phrase were to apply to everyone then it would be meaningless; it would be just another word for "men."

Let us consider how this is revealed in the Bible. The children of Israel thought of themselves as the children of God while they were in Egypt. Insofar as they believed they were the children of God, they decided the Egyptians were not.

After the Lord Jesus was called the Son of God, those who received Him were called the children of God.

> But as many as received him, to them gave he power to become the sons of God (John 1:12).

Believers were not children of God at the beginning, but they became so. We invite everyone to read the Bible. Undoubtedly many who are not believers read the Bible. We invite everyone to come to our church services, and many people who come are not believers. We encourage them to join in the Lord's Prayer, and together we say, "Our Father." It is surprising how many, on that basis, feel they belong among believers.

However, the New Testament magnified God as the Father

of those who believe in Him through Jesus Christ. ". . . neither knoweth any man the Father, save the Son, and he to whomsoever the Son will reveal him" (Matt. 11:27; see also Luke 10:22). Every time we see the word *Father* referring to God, we need to think of the Lord Jesus Christ as the "Son" of God.

Many seem to have the idea that because God created everything He is the "Father" of everything, but the Bible does not say this. It is true that God created everything; but when we use the word *Father* we are referring particularly to God's relationship with Jesus Christ His Son and to His relationship with those who put their trust in Him. Some apparently have begun to use the words *Father* and *child* when referring to the goodness and mercy of God and His giving benefits to the world, as a Father would give to his children. These people use the phrase "because God is the giver of every good and perfect gift" as a basis to speak of God as the Father, because a father gives good gifts to his child. Actually, the word *Father* in the Bible refers to the one who begets; and the Bible, in the New Testament, carefully uses the word *child* for those who are born again. They are "the children of God."

Inasmuch as God has provided whatever anyone has, it may seem to some that He is Father to whomsoever He gives anything. This line of thought holds that all men are His children, and so they are brothers of each other. But it is those who believe in Him and are begotten by Him and by His Word who are truly His children. He is their Father, and because they are His children, they are brothers of one another. Because this distinction has not been kept in mind in recent years there has arisen the general idea of the universal fatherhood of God and the universal brotherhood of man. Many have enbraced this idea, and it seems almost rude to question its validity. Actually believers want to share the blessing of God with everyone, but everyone is eligible for this blessing. The Scripture is very plain:

> But as many as received him, to them gave he power to become the sons of God (John 1:12).

This truth is implied clearly by Paul.

> And it shall come to pass, that in the place where it was said unto them, Ye are not my people; there shall they be called the children of the living God (Rom. 9:26).

Do you think this means everyone? Or can you see it means certain people? The very fact that they are called "the children of the living God" indicates this is different from what they were called before.

> [Isaiah] also crieth concerning Israel, Though the number of the children of Israel be as the sand of the sea, a remnant shall be saved (Rom. 9:27).

Here it is stated a remnant will be saved. This means that only some people will be saved: the children of God.

> And as [Isaiah] said before, Except the Lord of Sabaoth had left us a seed, we had been as [Sodom,] and been made like unto Gomorrah (Rom. 9:29).

The Lord left Israel a seed. Notice He did not make all Israel a harvest. This does not mean everyone in Israel belonged to Him, but only a seed, just a few out of the group as a whole. And many Gentiles will receive a blessing that Israel has not received.

> What shall we say then? That the Gentiles, which followed not after righteousness, have attained to righteousness, even the righteousness which is of faith. But Israel, which followed after the law of righteousness, hath not attained to the law of righteousness (Rom. 9:30,31).

Should we call both Jews and Gentiles children? If we called both of them children, the word would be meaningless. If we use the word *children* for those who belong to God and have the righteousness of God, we must give it to the Gentiles; otherwise there will be confusion.

> Wherefore? Because they sought it not by faith, but as it were by the works of the law. For they stumbled at that stumblingstone; as it is written, Behold, I lay in [Zion] a stumblingstone and rock of offence: and whosoever believeth on him shall not be ashamed (Rom. 9:32,33).

What about he who does not believe on Christ? That person should be ashamed. It is written "whosoever believeth on him shall not be ashamed." But about those who do not believe, the Scripture says:

> He that hath the Son hath life; and he that hath not the Son of God hath not life (1 John 5:12).

Shall we call all men "children of God"? It is true that God is good at all times to all men. But to say that this goodness of God makes all men agreeable and obedient to Him is not true. There are people who despise the goodness of God and who even despise the blood of Jesus Christ and trample it underfoot. How could anyone call them the children of God? Reserve the phrase "the children of God" for those who belong to Him through the Lord Jesus Christ.

God Almighty said, "This is my beloved Son. . . . Hear ye him" (Matt. 17:5). Those who believe in this beloved Son are the children of God.

Chapter 41

THE MISTAKE OF THE JEWS

(Romans 10:1-4)

Do you realize that being sincere will not help a person reach his desired destination if he is on the wrong road?

> For they being ignorant of God's righteousness, and going about to establish their own righteousness, have not submitted themselves unto the righteousness of God (Rom. 10:3).

In these words the apostle Paul indicates the operation of the grace of God in the gospel. He shows how certain people can miss it even though they are good people. When God calls man to Himself it is because He has provided a way to save him. If man does not come, the call is not operative. The call of God is not a long-range announcement to the whole universe that He will save everyone, allowing them in the meantime to go about their own business. The call of God is direct and personal. Those who respond will be given something they could never earn nor achieve on their own.

The gospel is humbling to man's pride. Man is asked to come and receive it from God, instead of trying to do it himself. It is true that this call of God is critical of man's efforts and abilities. Whoever receives it has to admit he is not good enough to earn it. It is also true that the gospel exalts Christ as Savior, making Him essential for salvation. A good, moral man may be tempted to try to achieve righteousness himself, confident that he can be good enough. This is a real danger. Jesus said with reference to entering into the kingdom of God that the rich will find it hard to enter; they will be tempted because of their riches to try to qualify on their own.

When Paul preached, he often thought of his kinsmen, the Jews. He realized some of them were good, moral, and wise, but he knew they were wrong in their procedures. They were trying to achieve righteousness themselves. When witnesses state that the Bible teaches there is none righteous, no, not one, many persons are inclined to think this is exaggerated. But the Lord solemnly declared that this was the truth.

In this portion of Romans we can see again that Paul is truly burdened for his own kindred. As we read and reflect on Romans 10:1-3 we may understand that the Jew is an example of men who know about God, and who want the blessing of God, but who go about receiving it the wrong way.

> Brethren, my heart's desire and prayer to God for Israel is, that they might be saved. For I bear them record that they have a zeal of God, but not according to knowledge (Rom. 10:1,2).

The Jews really tried to do what was right in God's sight, but they went about it in the wrong way.

> For they being ignorant of God's righteousness, and going about to establish their own righteousness, have not submitted themselves unto the righteousness of God (Rom. 10:3).

The longer they followed their own course, trying to establish their own righteousness, the further astray they went.

> For Christ is the end of the law for righteousness to every one that believeth (Rom. 10:4).

Accepting Christ means accepting Him as Savior. The believer no longer works to be saved; Christ will save him. He no longer tries to pay his way out, Christ has done it for him. Salvation is offered as a gift.

In this passage Paul describes the unhappy plight of many zealous people who try to do good works to get the blessing of God, but they make the mistake of going about it incorrectly. You may ask, what could they have done? They could have trusted God and then God would be working in them. This is the great truth in the gospel: God working in the believer to will and to do of His good pleasure.

The sobering aspect about all this is that it will apply to people who, compared to others, are good people. They help others and often take part in church and civic programs. But, while all their activity may be good, it is not good enough to save their souls. All they do can be done even better by those who respond to the grace of God which works within the heart. If a person has Christ Jesus in him, he will share in the worship of God, and he will share in service to his fellow man better than he ever could on his own, because it would be coming from the Lord. Because such grace comes from the Lord, God is pleased to give it to those who believe in Christ Jesus.

Chapter 42

THE WORD OF FAITH

(Romans 10:5-10)

Can you understand that when a man deals with himself properly he can be blessed of God to the uttermost?

> If thou shalt confess with thy mouth the Lord Jesus, and shalt believe in thine heart that God hath raised him from the dead, thou shalt be saved (Rom. 10:9).

These words constitute one of the great gospel promises of Scripture. Paul continues to discuss the difference between trying to save yourself and receiving the salvation already prepared for you. For example, to cross a lake you can either row across or let an outboard motor push your boat to the other side, in which event you would probably get there sooner. You would certainly be much fresher when you reach the other side. Paul uses the word *righteousness* to cover what he has in mind for the objective of the individual, and there is such a thing as seeking this righteousness by works.

> For Moses describeth the righteousness which is of the law, That the man which doeth those things shall live by them (Rom. 10:5).

When a person undertakes something, everything depends on how much and how long the effort is continued. This will determine how effectively it will be accomplished.

> The word is nigh thee, even in thy mouth, and in thy heart: that is, the word of faith, which we preach; That if thou shalt confess with thy mouth the Lord Jesus, and shalt believe in thine heart that God hath raised him from the dead, thou shalt be saved. For with the heart man believeth unto righteousness; and with the mouth confession is made unto salvation (Rom. 10:8-10).

All that is needed will be given to you — in this way righteousness is received by faith. Romans 10:5 indicated how righteousness can be sought by works; these verses show how it is received by faith. When a person seeks righteousness by works, everything depends on the persistence and effectiveness of his efforts. Romans 10:9 indicates how righteousness is received by faith: everything depends on believing in God, who will do it. When righteousness is sought by works there is never a point where the person can be certain righteousness is secured. If I am seeking salvation by my works, I have to be persistent; and there is one thing I know about myself: I can't keep it up. I am just not able to. I have to take time out and rest.

If my salvation depends on my works I have the uneasy feeling I have rested too much, or I have not done all I could have done. I never reach a point of assured achievement, because the grace of God is obviously operative, and I can be saved only while it is being practiced. When I stop practicing, all is lost. When I receive righteousness by faith, by committing myself to Him, I have the immediate assurance it will be done, for it is God who does it. And we know about God: He is the Keeper of Israel; He neither slumbers nor sleeps. What God does is done right. My salvation will actually be accomplished, and this assurance comes when I receive righteousness by faith.

When He was here on earth our Lord pointed out that under certain conditions thieves, publicans, and harlots would enter the kingdom of heaven before many so-called righteous people. Why would that happen? Because many "righteous" people try to get there by themselves, and they will never make it, for there is none righteous, no, not one. Whereas many unrighteous people know they are not what they ought to be, and because of this they are ready to receive the gospel as it is presented.

In a congregation a person yields his life to the Lord, and while he may not have a perfect life, he is happy. In spite of calamity or lack of money he is happy in the Lord. He is happy because he is trusting in God. He believes that God will work all things together for good to them that love Him. He does not have anything, but God has everything. In contrast there are people who try to live good lives and work hard. They feel everything depends on themselves, and so they never feel sure about their salvation. When you ask them if they are going to heaven, the best they can say is they certainly "hope so." All they can do is hope it turns out all right, because it depends on them and they might falter. That is why our Lord could say that many publicans and harlots would enter the kingdom of heaven before many righteous people, because they receive it from God. They trust in Him.

This is the word of faith which we preach:

> That if thou shalt confess with thy mouth the Lord Jesus, and shalt believe in thine heart that God hath raised him from the dead, thou shalt be saved (Rom. 10:9).

Chapter 43

THE UNIVERSAL PROMISE

(Romans 10:11-13)

Do you understand why salvation produces the same results in every man? It is because it is a gift from the same Lord in each case.

> For whosoever shall call upon the name of the Lord shall be saved (Rom. 10:13).

In these words the apostle Paul expresses confidence that has been comforting assurance to many souls. If God is no respecter of persons and has almighty power, and if salvation is a gift, then anyone can be saved. There is, however, a special slant to this revelation as we see in verse 11: "For the scripture saith, Whosoever believeth on him shall not be ashamed." Faith in Christ does not make a person shameless; but anyone believing in Him will never be embarrassed by lack of results. Believing in the Lord Jesus Christ will actually bring results. It is committing oneself to Him for help and for grace, enabling the soul to obey God; and no believer has ever been disappointed by a lack of power.

When a person believes in Christ he will commit himself to Him and receive the help and grace he needs to obey God.

> For there is no difference between the Jew and the Greek: for the same Lord over all is rich unto all that call upon him (Rom. 10:12).

Suppose in traveling on a road made muddy by heavy rains, a few cars slip from the highway into the ditch. One of the cars is a large limousine, and it gets stuck in the mud. Another car stuck in the mud is a small economy car. Now when the tow truck comes along, both cars will be pulled out of the ditch. The limousine will get out of the mud just as surely as the little compact. Why? Because it is not the compact nor the limousine that does the work; it is the tow truck that pulls them out. "And whosoever believeth on him shall be saved." For the tow truck there is no difference between the limousine and the compact. The same Lord over all will be rich unto *all* who call upon Him. Think of the following illustration: two men want to get to the tenth floor. One of them is a strong athlete, while the other man is on crutches. But both will get to the tenth floor at the same moment, because of the elevator, which is no respecter of persons.

This is the wonder of the gospel! Being saved is not a reward for how much you do; being saved is of the power of God. It is of the Lord Jesus Christ, who once told the parable about a man who owned a vineyard and hired people to work in it. He told those he hired early in the morning that he would give them a certain amount of money. Two hours later he saw some people standing around, so he hired them and offered them also a certain amount of money. At noon he saw other people without work, and he brought them in to work half a day for a certain amount of money. Later in the day he saw more men standing idle, so he hired them to work and promised each one a certain amount of money.

At the end of the day each worker received his promised wage and found it was just the same as that of the others. Of course, they wondered why they all received the same amount. But note, each received what he was promised. Many feel that those who do more deserve more than the others. In a sense this is true, but the Lord is teaching us that our reward is not dependent on what we do. The secret of the parable is that the pay was not earned; it was actually a gift. So it is with salvation. It is not something someone achieves: it is something a person receives. This is humbling. No doubt this is why some people do not like it, but it is a glorious truth, because the weak can be received as readily as the strong.

Chapter 44

THE NATURE OF FAITH

(Romans 10:14-21)

Do you know the difference between faith and make-believe?

> So then faith cometh by hearing, and hearing by the word of God (Rom. 10:17).

I wonder if everyone understands what saving faith really is. I often have the feeling that many think faith is believing anything they want to believe, yet still qualifying for blessing. They feel they can believe anything and if they truly do believe it, that is all that is required.

Certainly there is an element of volition in faith, so to an extent a person does choose what he wants to believe. This is the only way we can understand why some people believe as they do. Some people believe the most ridiculous things. But a person can decide to believe anything he wants to believe, and this is what I mean by "make-believe." This differs from what we understand about the saving faith of the gospel.

When one says that a person may believe anything he wants to, then faith becomes some sort of pressure or strength which functions as a mental exercise on his part, a kind of "plus" ingredient in his life and work. The person may put his time into his belief and then believe it will work all right if he "squeezes" it some. But this is not valid.

To truly have faith, there must be some expressed promise to be believed. If you wanted to believe that you would meet me at the church at 11 o'clock, would there be any way you could really believe I would be there at that time? Yes, if I told you I would be there. But if you just made up your own mind that we would meet at 11 o'clock, that does not hold any power. If there is no promise, it might not happen. In order to believe, there must be some expressed promise. If I say I will be at the church at 11 o'clock and you hear me say it, you may then believe it or not. If you believe it, you will expect that I will be there, and you will make your plans accordingly.

Your belief that I am going to meet you does not get me there. I will go because *I* decide to. Believing on your part may get *you* there, but it does not make *me* go. In other words, simply believing does not make anything happen. It merely puts you in line to have it happen to you.

All this can be seen in Romans 10:14-21, where the idea is brought out that believing is not something vague and indefinite. I recently heard about a person described as a believer. I was told "she does not believe in the God of the Bible and she does not believe in Jesus Christ, but she believes." What does she believe? People believe all kinds of things. Some believe that an idol made of wood can help them; and there are people who believe horseshoes will bring good luck. Others believe in signs and omens of various kinds. There are many things a person can believe, but these may not be saving things. Believing unto salvation means a person must believe in the Lord Jesus Christ.

> How then shall they call on him in whom they have not believed? and how shall they believe in him of whom they have not heard? and how shall they hear without a preacher? (Rom. 10:14).

Apparently, something is to be preached. What will be preached? The promises of God from the Scripture. Someone who is going to preach will interpret passages of Scripture; he will not expound on his own ideas.

This passage emphasizes the whole matter of God's salvation. His plan is revealed in His Word in the form of promises. The true meaning of saving faith is to accept as true and valid whatever God has promised in His Word. One needs to hear the gospel preached; and the testimony of others who have believed and been blessed will strengthen a person to believe.

In verse 18 Paul seems to claim that communication has been made to all people. According to verse 18 this was apparently done in nature.

> But I say, Have they not heard? Yes verily, their sound went into all the earth, and their words unto the ends of the world (Rom. 10:18).

This is a quotation from the Old Testament (Ps. 19:4) about the natural creation which shows forth the glory of God. Believers know about that. Romans 10:19 and 20 reveal that God worked to show people His ways to encourage them to believe in Him. And finally, in verse 21 the revelation came in personal experience:

> All day long I have stretched forth my hands unto a disobedient and gainsaying people (Rom. 10:21).

If they had ever stopped being disobedient and had obeyed, if they had stopped arguing and had accepted what was said, they would have had all of this revelation.

There really seems to be no excuse for anyone in Israel failing to understand the plan of salvation and committing himself to it. This is the significance of this whole portion of Scripture. Paul wants to make it plain that God will save anyone: "whosoever believes in him." Apparently the Scriptures were given to this end:

> So then faith cometh by hearing, and hearing by the word of God (Rom. 10:17).

Let me remind you: in the Word of God there are many promises. Some of these promises are stated explicitly, and sometimes a promise is shown in an event. God's promise in Christ Jesus is "whosoever believeth in me shall never perish but have everlasting life." When you are given such a promise, and you respond to it, you will find it valid. Any other kind of faith is what I call "make-believe." When one makes up what he thinks God will say or do, there is no promise in that. God's promise depends on what He has revealed; and what He has revealed He will perform. Because that is true, there is no excuse for anyone who has heard the gospel not to put his trust in it.

Chapter 45

THE RIGHTEOUSNESS OF GOD

(Romans 10:3-13)

Do you understand what is meant in the Bible by "the righteousness of God"?

Righteousness is not the kind of word we ordinarily use. I suspect many days go by that we never use it. When we speak of the righteousness of God we are not talking about some characteristic of God Himself or a trait of His own personality. Instead we refer to righteousness in a human being which comes from God.

Righteousness is not something tangible. A person cannot get a bag of it, nor can he carry it around in a box. The truth is, there can be righteous words and acts, righteous looks, and a righteous attitude, but there is no such item as "righteousness." Actually, the word *righteousness* refers to a quality or a condition of something. When something is right, it is righteous; when a man is right he is righteous. Right means to fit some standard exactly.

When we use the phrase "exactly like God" we refer to something that is "righteous" in God's sight; it is right with God, straight. Everything straight and upright is like God — righteous; anything else is wicked. The word *wicked* in the Hebrew means "devious" or "deviating." The Book of Romans deals with the problem of making straight the sinful, the deviating, crooked one; making him right with God.

This is also the meaning of the word *just*. We speak about a man's conduct as just when his actions are what they should be. It is because they are "exactly according to" that they are "just" —*just* means "exactly equal to." If a man is evil but wants to be right, we tell him to "straighten up." The gospel points out that a human being can, in God through Jesus Christ, receive the grace that will make him "right," "straight up," "exactly according to" God.

Here is an amazing truth: if a person receives the Lord Jesus Christ as He is presented in the gospel, something will happen to cause him to become right with God. We call this "the righteousness of God" because it occurs through no effort on the person's part. This is what Paul meant when he said, "Therein is the righteousness of God revealed from faith to faith." In the gospel we are told how a crooked, devious man can be straightened out, can become right in the sight of God. This is not so much merely a pattern of conduct, nor does this refer specifically to the things that person will do; it refers to an attitude he will have. If the attitude is a willingness on his part to obey, such a man will look into the face of God and say, "Here am I. Send me," and "Speak, Lord, for thy servant heareth." This is the attitude God desires; it makes the person right with Him.

In becoming a believer a person does not need to experience a long, drawn-out argument about right and wrong. The person is brought face to face with the truth about his conduct, and if he is honest he will say, "I am a sinner." If he has any knowledge of the gospel, he will know "the soul that sinneth, it shall die." But now he learns that by believing in Christ he can be forgiven, and he can be saved. By His grace and His mercy, through His Holy Spirit, God works in that man, giving him an entirely new view. Every man in Christ Jesus is a "new creature." The Lord God will incline him to do the will of God and this will make him right in God's sight.

When Paul says that the Jew missed this righteousness, he is noting a common mistake among religious people — that of trying to qualify oneself, trying to be good. The Jews were religiously trained so they knew what was in the Bible. They had a zeal for God, but it was not according to knowledge, nor was it intelligent, because they were attempting to establish their own righteousness by their own efforts. Actually being right with God is not a matter of something a person does by himself; it is something God does in him when he commits his life to Him. It is not what he does outwardly, but it is an inward attitude of seeking God's pleasure. One will be inclined this way when he receives Jesus Christ as his own Lord and Savior.

Chapter 46

THE REMNANT

(Romans 11:1-6)

Do you realize that the majority is not always right?

> Even so then at this present time also there is a remnant according to the election of grace (Rom. 11:5).

There is a procedure to be followed in communicating the gospel among men. When the promises of God are set forth in preaching and teaching, they generate faith. Faith is believing what has been revealed. But this faith is not automatic. It does not follow that if a preacher faithfully preaches the truth everyone who hears him will receive it. The response is individual: some listen and some do not.

When Jesus Christ was on earth there were some who believed in Him and some who did not. This gospel is not always popularly received; it cannot always be counted on that the majority will receive it. It is said that Noah was a preacher of righteousness and that he preached for 120 years while the ark was being built, but the people of his day did not believe him. Jesus of Nazareth taught that the gate is straight and the way narrow that "leadeth unto life, and few there be that find it" (Matt. 7:14).

Many wonder whether or not we should accept the idea that only a minority will believe; but it is based on historic fact. At Kadesh-Barnea, under the leadership of Moses, twelve spies were sent out. When they returned to report, ten said the land could not be taken; but the ten were wrong. Two said it could be done with the help of God; they were right.

Paul emphasizes that there is a remnant, a few people who believe, even among the Jews, according to the election of grace. What he was facing is difficult for us to understand. He was one Jew standing out and preaching for Jesus Christ. The entire establishment of the Jews was against him. His prayer was that Israel might be saved. He noted that they had a zeal for God, but not according to knowledge. He points out here the fact that the Jews, the popular group who opposed his message, are missing the point. Resolutely he sustains his position.

Paul fears people might get the idea that God had failed with Israel; and here he argues that the promise was not a failure.

> I say then, Hath God cast away his people? God forbid. For I also am an Israelite, of the seed of Abraham, of the tribe of Benjamin. God hath not cast away his people which he foreknew. Wot ye not what the scripture saith of [Elijah]? how he maketh intercession to God against Israel, saying, Lord, they have killed thy prophets, and digged down thine altars; and I am left alone, and they seek my life. But what saith the answer of God unto him? I have reserved to myself seven thousand men, who have not bowed the knee to the image of Baal. Even so then at this present time also there is a remnant according to the election of grace (Rom. 11:1-5).

The promises made to Israel are being fulfilled in every Jew who believes. When Paul says, "God hath not cast away his people which he foreknew," he means that when a Jew believes, he is one of God's people. God did not cast them away. Those who believe in Him will be saved as in the time of Elijah, for example, there were seven thousand who belonged to God. These people were not members of the political establishment of Israel. They were secret believers, and even now there is a remnant.

The word *remnant* refers to the few true believers among widespread indifference. Each person must face God individually, and he must come to God even if no one else does. One should not be influenced by popular opinion. If he follows the crowd, he will not come to God. A person should not feel insignificant because he comes to God alone. One soul is as important to God as a whole community, but this is a viewpoint most human beings do not comprehend. We are individually responsible to God, and therefore we should forget about those around us and come to God willingly.

Chapter 47

THE BLINDNESS OF ISRAEL

(Romans 11:7-15)

Can you believe a person may be zealous about seeking the favor of God and at the same time be blind as to what God actually wants him to do?

> Israel hath not obtained that which he seeketh for; but the election hath obtained it, and the rest were blinded . . . unto this day (Rom. 11:7,8).

This is a grave fact and none of us should take it lightly. Earnest people can be wrong, and this should humble all of us. We all need to hear God's Word speak to us: "Let him that thinketh he standeth take heed lest he fall" (1 Cor. 10:12). This does not mean it is inevitable that anyone should fall. Those who humbly seek the mind of the Lord will be able to stand. It does not mean that anything unfair is being done to anyone. It is simply another reflection of the fact that the human heart is evil, desperately wicked, and not to be trusted, even in a sincere person.

When we say the human heart is wicked we do not mean it is always immoral or vulgar. We simply mean the human heart is devious; and this is what the Scripture calls sin. Paul points out that some who earnestly pursued what they thought was right actually were wrong. Paul uses himself as an example. As a young man he had served God with a clear conscience and believed he was doing right by persecuting Christ's followers. In one place he said, "I verily thought with myself, that I ought to do many things contrary to the name of Jesus of Nazareth" (Acts 26:9). It is never enough for anyone to say, "I meant well." In those words lies the road to disaster for many. Sincerity, while it is good, is not good enough.

In the following passage, which is extremely important, we

should not gloat but think soberly about ourselves. We could be wrong. Just being sincere does not make us right. "Israel hath not obtained that which he seeketh for; but the election hath obtained it." Some have accepted the grace of God but the rest were blinded. Who were the rest? Paul described them when he wrote:

> For they being ignorant of God's righteousness, and going about to establish their own righteousness, have not submitted themselves unto the righteousness of God (Rom. 10:3).

The origin of their condition is clearly set forth:

> God hath given them the spirit of slumber, eyes that they should not see, and ears that they should not hear; unto this day (Rom. 11:8).

Paul now raises the question in verse 11: "I say then, Have they stumbled that they should fall?" This is a way of asking, Were they allowed to blunder just to be destroyed? Did God give them the spirit of slumber because He wanted to destroy them? Then this phrase occurs again, "God forbid." As mentioned before, this is better translated as something like "Let it not be said." ". . . but rather through their fall salvation is come unto the Gentiles, for to provoke them to jealousy."

Because of the Jews' rejection of Christ and their subsequent distress, the door was opened to the Gentiles, who came and were blessed. Now the Jews must compare their own unblessed state with that of the blessed Gentiles. Something like this can be seen when some people in the church actually feel chagrin because there are those who, since their parents were believers and they have always gone to a Christian church, still do not seem to be sure in their hearts about the Lord, while other persons who never used to go to church and whose families did not attend, now have accepted the Lord Jesus Christ and are happy. Still, the first group may not feel certain that they are going to heaven, and this would cause them to compare themselves with the others. Paul points out:

> For I speak to you Gentiles, inasmuch as I am the apostle of the Gentiles, I magnify mine office: if by any means I may provoke to emulation them which are my flesh, and might save some of them. For if the casting away of them be the reconciling of the world, what shall the receiving of them be, but life from the dead? (Rom. 11:13-15).

Paul is saying that even though these people in their foolishness have been wrong, they were sincere. They could be won to the Lord. He tries to win them by telling them how the Gentiles have been blessed.

Chapter 48

THE BREAKING OFF OF ISRAEL

(Romans 11:16-25)

Do you realize that persons brought up in the church can be lost?

> Because of unbelief they were broken off . . . (Rom. 11:20).

These are the words the apostle Paul uses when addressing the Jews. We will notice in these verses a sad fact that children from religious homes can be lost; on the other hand, children from ungodly, worldly homes can be saved. This does not mean that homes do not count, but they do not count for everything. Parents may provide a religious atmosphere and take their children to church, but if they do not actively work at bringing them to faith, their children may grow up in unbelief. However, parents who do not care about this may have children who go to Sunday school and church, where they hear the gospel preached, and they come to faith and are saved.

Paul uses the image of olive trees: he speaks of Israel as the tame olive tree and the Gentiles as the wild olive tree. (In our day we would say religious people represent the tame olive tree and worldly people the wild olive tree.) Next he declares the sober truth: Israel, a religious people, can miss the blessing of the gospel if they try to get by with being good enough in themselves; whereas, the Gentiles (worldly people) can receive the grace of God if they accept Jesus Christ. It could be illustrated like this: two men are cast from a boat at sea, one of whom can swim. A lifeboat is provided for them and the man who cannot swim gets into it, while the one who can swim refuses, and in attempting to swim the distance, he drowns.

Religious people can be overconfident because they want to do the right things, but their emphasis is wrong; whereas worldly people who are aware of their weakness may repent and receive the Lord Jesus Christ and walk in Him. Those who are in the Lord are saved and the people who are not are not saved, regardless of how good they may be. Because this is true, Paul suggests that these worldly people, having received Jesus Christ, could be tempted to feel proud since they have the advantage over religious people who are going on their own. Paul warns the Gentile converts against the danger of smugness.

> . . . and thou, being a wild olive tree, wert grafted in among them (Rom. 11:17).

This is a figure used to indicate the spiritual relationship established when a person accepts Jesus Christ. Such a believer is grafted in among other branches on the tree. When he becomes a believer he joins with Christ's people and enters into their fellowship. Elsewhere in the New Testament this fellowship is called "the church." Although a person may have been worldly, by believing in Jesus Christ he is counted like other believers and he bears fruit in the Lord.

> Boast not against the branches. But if thou boast, thou bearest not the root, but the root thee (Rom. 11:18).

Here is an earnest word to young believers who often have a tendency to become smug. In case any believer is tempted to boast, he should remember it is the root that is carrying him. He is not carrying the root.

> . . . because of unbelief they were broken off (Rom. 11:20).

This unbelief was not so much a matter of denial, or that they believed something else, as it was default. They did not believe at all. Because of their failure to even investigate it, they missed the blessing. They did not exercise faith in Jesus Christ, nor did they receive Him as Savior. It appears that some could receive Him as Savior, but could fail to enter into consecration by neglecting to follow through.

> Be not high-minded, but fear (Rom. 11:20).

This is a serious matter in spiritual experience. We should always bear in mind: "God resisteth the proud and giveth grace to the humble." There is goodness from God upon those who continue to believe, but there is severity upon those who do not work at it. A garden can bear weeds if you do not work it. If you do work it, you can have fruit. God produces the fruit.

Romans 11:23 gives a wonderful truth: "And they also, if they abide not still in unbelief, shall be grafted in: for God is able to graft them in again." God is able to graft people in again. Even if the garden goes to weeds this year, it could bear a good crop next year. Those who have lived a long time in their own goodness and missed the gospel because they have not received Christ are yet able to receive Him. So hear the Word concerning this and if you are blessed in the providence of God, be humble and obedient to Him by receiving Jesus Christ as Savior and Lord.

Chapter 49

THE WISDOM OF GOD

(Romans 11:26-36)

Do you realize that God is able to overrule in all things to bring His will to pass?

> O the depth of the riches both of the wisdom and knowledge of God! how unsearchable are his judgments, and his ways past finding out! (Rom. 11:33).

In Romans 11:26 we read a statement of confidence: "And so all Israel shall be saved." This is a strange statement to make at this point. Paul has just been talking about Jews and Gentiles. What does he mean when he speaks about "all Israel shall be saved"? It is important for us to know that "Israel" does not refer to any national group. This is not the nation of Israel that is going to be saved, nor is it the race of the Israelite people (the Hebrews, the descendants of Abraham). "Israel" here refers to the *spiritual* descendants of Abraham. In chapter 9 Paul noted that they were not all Abraham who are of Abraham. "In Isaac shall thy seed be called": not even all of Isaac, but "in" Isaac shall his seed be "called." So the spiritual believers — those who receive the promise given to Abraham — are the true seed of Abraham. This should be kept in mind. All who believe in the Lord Jesus Christ, whether Jew or Gentile, will be saved.

Paul writes another strange statement:

> As concerning the gospel, they are enemies for your sakes: but as touching the election, they are beloved for the fathers' sakes (Rom. 11:28).

I am inclined to think that where the word *gospel* is used Paul is referring to the public preaching of God in Christ. Israel as a company of people were enemies, hostile to the public preaching of the gospel. They resisted Paul when he preached.

But in the "election," we have both Jews and Gentiles, whoever is a believer. At this point I think it refers to the individual and the inward, personal call of the promises and grace of God. Concerning these individual believers, "beloved for the fathers' sakes," each is a child of Abraham.

> For as ye in times past have not believed God, yet have now obtained mercy through their unbelief: even so have these also now not believed, that through your mercy they also may obtain mercy (Rom. 11:30,31).

Through the kindness of Gentile believers the gospel was preached even to these Jews, not holding anything against them because they as Jews had at one time turned away. Those who believe should give everyone a chance to believe, graciously, humbly, and mercifully, showing them that in Christ Jesus they can be saved.

Paul refers back to the first three chapters of Romans and to the "natural" people: Gentiles who did not know God, and Jews who did know God and the Scriptures but were sinners who needed to be saved in Jesus Christ.

> For God hath concluded them all in unbelief, that he might have mercy upon all (Rom. 11:32).

The mercy of God is that in Christ Jesus anyone can be saved.

> O the depth of the riches both of the wisdom and knowledge of God! how unsearchable are his judgments, and his ways past finding out! For who hath known the mind of the Lord? or who hath been his counsellor? Or who hath first given to him, and it shall be recompensed unto him again? For of him, and through him, and to him, are all things: to whom be glory for ever. Amen (Rom. 11:33-36).

In this frame of mind Paul brings the whole problem of Jews and Gentiles together unto God. I may point out in this connection that sometimes we say that the gospel is for the down-and-outer and that is gloriously true. But the gospel is also for the up-and-outer! We should remember this. The gospel can save anyone, no matter how bad he is; and the gospel can save anyone, no matter how good he is. Whosoever will believe in the Lord Jesus Christ shall not perish, but have everlasting life.

Chapter 50

A LIVING SACRIFICE

(Romans 12:1-2)

Do you have any idea what a person who wants to serve God should do first?

> I beseech you therefore, brethren, by the mercies of God, that ye present your bodies a living sacrifice, holy, acceptable unto God, which is your reasonable service (Rom. 12:1).

Paul places on all believers the responsibility of responding to God in service. This applies only to believers. When boarding a plane there is often a sign displayed at a certain point which reads, Passengers Only; likewise, at this point in our discussion, we should remember that what we will be reading in Romans is For Believers Only. Those who believe are the ones who will endeavor to follow the admonitions. These verses will guide the reader to realize the blessings of God and to bring to pass what God has in mind for him. Salvation (which is the work of the Lord Jesus Christ) is effectual only when there is obedience.

> I beseech you therefore, brethren, by the mercies of God, that ye present your bodies a living sacrifice (Rom. 12:1).

The word *beseech* can be variously translated, but it implies urgent exhortation. Notice how the word *brethren* is used here: Paul is writing to his brothers, his fellow believers.

When Paul says "by the mercies of God" he is referring to everything he wrote in the first eleven chapters. Put together they would read something like this: justification, which God will do for you; the providence of God, having God watch over you; and sanctification, how God will actually incline you to do His will and work in you that which is pleasing in His sight. These are the mercies of God. God has done and will continue to do wonderful things for you.

In view of the wonderful things that God has done for them, Paul now urges believers to "present your bodies a living sacrifice, holy, acceptable unto God, which is your reasonable service." It would certainly be in Paul's mind how the worshipers brought sacrifices to God. One characteristic of a lamb is that it "before [the] shearer is dumb" (Isa. 53:7). At the same time, there is no reason to suppose that the sacrificial sheep or oxen were glad to be killed. In the same way do you think I would enjoy yielding myself to be crucified? Think of the Garden of Gethsemane when our Lord sweated, as it were, great drops of blood as He faced the time when He would be separated from His Father in death. To be a living sacrifice we are to present our bodies, to yield and deny ourselves even unto death.

The word *holy* has the same meaning as the English word *wholly*. It means without reservation, altogether committed, "acceptable unto God, which is your reasonable service." It is a way of saying: If you belong to Him, use your common sense and turn yourself over to Him. He has purchased you, therefore He owns you.

> And be not conformed to this world (Rom. 12:2).

Do not let this world shape you the way it wants to shape you under its pressures.

> . . . but be ye transformed by the renewing of your mind (Rom. 12:2).

This means renewing your mind once and for all, not a temporary renewing day by day. The believer will have a new mind in Christ Jesus.

> . . . that ye may prove what is that good, and acceptable, and perfect, will of God (Rom. 12:2).

There is a sense in which every day the believer should deny himself and be crucified. As he is crucified every day, every day he will be raised from the dead. It is impossible to be raised into the newness of life unless the believer has died with the Lord. If every day he is willing to die, he can expect every day to be raised. In this manner he may show by the results in his life what is the good and acceptable and perfect will of God.

Chapter 51

MEMBERS ONE OF ANOTHER

(Romans 12:3-8)

Do you realize that every believer is personally involved with every other believer?

> For none of us liveth to himself, and no man dieth to himself (Rom. 14:7).

It is true that naturally we belong to each other as human beings, but this is especially true for believers. Whereas, for instance, when I drive in traffic I belong to the whole stream of traffic, spiritually speaking, I am involved with other believers because of the one Holy Spirit within us. Think of a tree: the smaller branches grow out from one limb and eventually cause the branches from another limb to move over. That is one way in which they are related to one another. Is it not also true that the life inside each branch is one living organism? It is not only a matter of outward adjustment. There is an inward reality that makes the whole tree with all its branches one living organism.

This clearly illustrates Paul's ideas. There is an inward unity involving all believers, and each believer also has an external relationship with eveyone, believer and nonbeliever. I conduct myself a certain way as far as non-Christians are concerned, but I have a certain inward relationship with other Christians. This will become more obvious as we follow Paul's thought.

> For I say, through the grace given unto me, to every man that is among you, not to think of himself more highly than he ought to think; but to think soberly, according as God hath dealt to every man the measure of faith (Rom. 12:3).

This is a straightforward, honest statement that tells believers not to think too much of themselves, for the sake of others.

Inwardly, believers want to get along with people, so Paul urges them to be careful what they think about themselves. Phillips' translation of this verse is: "As your spiritual teacher, I give this piece of advice to each one of you. Don't cherish exaggerated ideas of yourself or of your importance, but try to have a sane estimate of your capabilities by the light of the faith which God has given to you all." I should surely think something of myself. Under certain circumstances I should esteem myself. But I should think soberly and, as Phillips says, sanely.

> For as we have many members in one body, and all members have not the same office: so we, being many, are one body in Christ, and every one members one of another (Rom. 12:4,5).

Here Paul uses the body as an illustration: a person has hands, feet, ears, eyes, a nose, and a mouth. There are many members in the body, but all members do not have the same office. A person does one thing with his hands, another with his ears, and another with his eyes. In the same way we believers, being many, are one body in Christ. Phillips writes: "For just as you have many members in one physical body and those members differ in their function, so we though many in number compose one body in Christ and are all members one of another." But we should not overestimate ourselves.

> Having then gifts differing according to the grace that is given to us, whether prophecy, let us prophesy according to the proportion of faith (Rom. 12:6).

Phillips translates this verse: "Through the grace of God we have different gifts. If our gift be preaching, let us preach to the limit of our vision." Every believing parent preaches to his children. Preaching or prophesying is communicating the meaning of the Scripture. All kinds of questions might be asked and discussed, sometimes from curiosity but often because of genuine interest. Paul would tell you concerning your answers, don't say more than you know. What you don't see, don't say.

> Or ministry, let us wait on our ministering: or he that teacheth, on teaching; or he that exhorteth, on exhortation: he that giveth, let him do it with simplicity; he that ruleth, with diligence; he that soweth mercy, with cheerfulness (Rom. 12:7,8).

Phillips expresses the meaning of this passage thus:

> If it is serving others, let us concentrate on our service; if it is teaching, let us give all we have to our teaching; and if our gift be the stimulating of the faith of others let us set ourselves to it. Let the man who is called to give, give freely; let the man who wields authority think of his responsibility; and let the man who feels sympathy for his fellows act cheerfully (Rom. 12:7,8 Phillips).

Believers should be sure that they do only their part and no more. We often think of gifts with reference to their function. We say someone is gifted because he can do this, and another is gifted because she can do that; but Paul is here referring to the word *gift* with emphasis on its origin, where it comes from. If God has enabled the believer to do certain things, giving him the privilege and opportunity to do those things, he must be careful not to stretch himself to do more than he knows. He should be humble.

Chapter 52

INSTRUCTION

(Romans 12:9-16)

Can you understand how a person who wants to do the will of God would need guidance and instruction?

> Abhor that which is evil; cleave to that which is good (Rom. 12:9).

In our last study we spoke about the gifts that are given to believers. When we speak about a gift we realize this is not only an inward capacity; many times it is actually an opportunity. One may have special inward gifts for teaching: a clear mind, ready speech, good illustrations, and a pleasant voice. All of these things would help, but if one does not have pupils, he cannot be a teacher. The gift of teaching, therefore, includes the opportunity to teach; the gift of preaching includes an opportunity to preach. The gift of giving is fine if you have something to give, but many do not have the gift of giving because they have nothing to give.

A person eager to do God's will needs to be told what to do. This person will welcome instruction. In all conduct, in everything a person does, there are always two elements present: the disposition to want to do something and the skill in knowing how to do it. Paul has dwelt on those matters which would incline believers to obey God, and now in chapters 12-15 he points out how they should obey. "Let love be without dissimulation" (12:9). Remember, love is not sentiment; love is doing something on behalf of others. Now Paul is saying that when we do something for others, let there be no pretense or hypocrisy. Let love be genuine. "Abhor that which is evil; cleave to that which is good." Wouldn't you think everyone would be able to do that? It may seem strange, but some cannot. There are people who are inwardly disposed to be kind and gracious, but who do not have good sense about people. The word *abhor* means "turn away from." It includes an element of hate. This principle could be stated as follows: Hate that which is evil; cleave to that which is good. The good should be desired. There are people who are not good, and Paul would say, "Turn away!" And there are others who radiate goodness. Paul would say, "Cling to them!"

> Be kindly affectioned one to another with brotherly love (Rom. 12:10).

"Kindly affectioned" has to do with a person's attitude. The believer should let his attitude toward another person be kind. Some people genuinely care about others, yet when they deal with them, they are unkind. This may happen among parents many times. One would think some parents hate their children by the way they treat them. Brotherly love is not based on esteem or preference; it is based on the fact that someone is a brother. He may not be attractive, but he is your brother. When you say "love," it does not mean you have warm feelings toward him: it means you help him.

> . . . in honour preferring one another (Rom. 12:10).

This is not "in *judgment* preferring one another." The other person may not be as wise as you. This does not mean "in *esteem* preferring one another." The other person may not be as estimable as you are. But in *honor*, in paying attention to him, give him first place.

> Not slothful in business; fervent in spirit; serving the Lord (Rom. 12:11).

This verse says, Don't be lazy. Don't be lukewarm. Get on fire for the things of the Lord!

> Rejoicing in hope; patient in tribulation; continuing instant in prayer (Rom. 12:12).

Paul does not mean we are to rejoice about *everything*, but we as believers should rejoice about the things God promises because they will turn out wonderfully. We should be patient in persevering. No matter how much trouble we meet, we should stay with it until it is finished. We should always be ready to pray, "distributing to the necessity of saints." We need not assume responsibility for the whole community; we may not have that much money. But we do have a special responsibility to other believers. ". . . given to hospitality" (Rom. 12:13). We should always be gracious in sharing what we have with those who are in need. "Bless them which persecute you" (Rom. 12:14). We should do this not because others persecute us but *in spite of* the fact that they persecute us. ". . . bless, and curse not."

Chapter 53

EXHORTATION

(Romans 12:17-21)

Is there ever a time when you should tell someone what he ought to do?

> Bless them which persecute you: bless, and curse not (Rom. 12:14).

Paul, in these verses, is telling believers what to do, applying the godly attitudes he discussed in earlier verses in this chapter. We believers should bless those who persecute us, not *because* they persecute us but *in spite of* this. We have been blessed of God and we in turn should bless others. What if others do not bless us? Men did not bless the Lord Jesus Christ. What if others do not treat us right? They did not treat Him right. What if people do not help us? They did not help Him; yet He came to help them. So believers bless those who persecute them in spite of such behavior. Every action believers take is constructive, for the benefit of others, not destructive to hurt anyone.

> Rejoice with them that do rejoice, and weep with them that weep (Rom. 15:15).

This is a simple way of saying, "Be sympathetic." Do you realize why it is so hard for me to rejoice with people who are having great joy in their hearts? It is because of myself. If I could forget myself, I could rejoice with them. While I am selfish I will not be able to do it.

> Be of the same mind one toward another. Mind not high things, but condescend to men of low estate. Be not wise in your own conceits (Rom. 12:16).

The believer should treat everyone alike. He should pay attention not only to those who are winning, but also to those who are losing. Being interested in and attracted to a brilliant person would be natural,.but to give each person his place, regardless of who he is, would be the spiritual way. Believers are being warned it is a good thing to be "foolish" in themselves but wise in the Lord.

> Recompense to no man evil for evil. Provide things honest in the sight of all men (Rom. 12:17).

These are simple admonitions. A believer should not seek retaliation. He should not try to get even with people. Instead he should act honestly. He should be thoughtful of other people and act accordingly. He is led to be reverent toward God. Thus, he will worship God and go to church. He wants to know the will of God so he reads the Bible.

> If it be possible, as much as lieth in you, live peaceably with all men (Rom. 12:18).

A person cannot control everything. Another person may not be peaceable, but the believer can be. He should not take offense no matter what others do, and he should not give offense. The believer should seek peace with all men and pursue it. Yet some responsibility lies in the other fellow, so the believer may not be able to be at peace with everyone.

> Dearly beloved, avenge not yourselves, but rather give place unto wrath: for it is written, Vengeance is mine; I will repay, saith the Lord (Rom. 12:19).

The believer should never take up a weapon in self-defense nor try to give the other fellow his dues, even if the other person has it coming to him. The believer should turn his case over to God and leave it in His hands. This is difficult to do because believers are often afraid that God will be too easy on that person.

> Therefore if thine enemy hunger, feed him; if he thirst, give him drink: for in so doing thou shalt heap coals of fire on his head. Be not overcome of evil, but overcome evil with good (Rom. 12:20,21).

This is how the believer should live. The evil that people do may sometimes provoke him. When someone does something unkind to him, he feels like doing something unkind back to that person, but instead he should do something kind. This is not easy but it will be good for him, and God will bless him.

Chapter 54

SUBJECT TO RULERS

(Romans 13:1-7)

Do you think a believer should always obey the laws of the land?

> Let evey soul be subject unto the higher powers (Rom. 13:1).

This is a much-discussed problem among us today. Should a Christian obey the laws of the land? Should he consider himself to be under the control of the local authorities? Many will argue that Peter and John set an example for us in the Book of Acts when they continued to preach even though they had been forbidden to do so. I want to point out that this is not the same kind of thing we read about in the papers. They were doing nothing for personal benefit. What they got out of it was a whipping, which they took gladly. They set an example for us in accepting the penalty.

Think back into the New Testament record. The Lord Jesus never disregarded any law, Roman or Jewish, or any regulations. He said it was fitting for us to submit ourselves and to fulfill all righteousness. There is not one case in the Gospels or in the Book of Acts where the disciples ever disobeyed civil law for personal interest. When the Lord Jesus was speaking about this to Pontius Pilate He said:

> My kingdom is not of this world: if my kingdom were of this world, then would my servants fight, that I should not be delivered to the Jews: but now is my kingdom not from hence (John 18:36).

Those words provide guidance for us. Because His kingdom was not of this world He accepted what the people did. What they did was against the law, but He never resisted. In keeping with His teaching to "render unto Caesar the things that are

Caesar's" we must be obedient to the laws of the land. Paul expounds this matter in the first six verses of Romans 13.

> Let every soul be subject unto the higher powers. For there is no power but of God: the powers that be are ordained of God (Rom. 13:1).

To resist the local government is to resist God because He has allowed this local government to exist.

> For rulers are not a terror to good works, but to the evil. Wilt thou then not be afraid of the power? do that which is good, and thou shalt have praise of the same: for he is the minister of God to thee for good. But if thou do that which is evil, be afraid; for he beareth not the sword in vain: for he is the minister of God, a revenger to execute wrath upon him that doeth evil (Rom. 13:3,4).

This is a rather labored exposition of the principle that government is designed for the common welfare of mankind, and as such it is entitled to our cooperative obedience. I recognize this is not always simple, because sometimes the traffic policeman is mistaken in what he says. Paul would tell you he should, however, be obeyed. As God-fearing people we will not have everything the way we want it here, but what is important is our testimony, and for us to be rebellious is bad. To be yielded is good.

> Wherefore ye must needs be subject, not only for wrath, but also for conscience sake. For for this cause pay ye tribute also: for they are God's ministers, attending continually upon this very thing. Render therefore to all their dues: tribute to whom tribute is due; custom to whom custom; fear to whom fear; honour to whom honour (Rom. 13:5-7).

This is a way of saying we must pay our taxes honestly. That is how the government is maintained financially, and we need government. Here, then, is the principle. When Ananias, the high priest, commanded that Paul be slapped, Paul rebuked the high priest. When it was questioned, Paul apologized and replied, ". . . it is written, Thou shalt not speak evil of the ruler of thy people" (Acts 23:5). A Christian should obey the laws of the land.

Chapter 55

FULFILLING THE LAW

(Romans 13:8-14)

Do you know any procedure a believer in God can follow in dealing with others that will always be right?

> Owe no man any thing, but to love one another: for he that loveth another hath fulfilled the law (Rom. 13:8).

This is the principle that should govern the conduct of every believer in God. Believers accept the responsibility to act carefully in dealing with others. The problems of conduct often involve fine lines of distinction, of judgment. God's will is what should be done. This is not always clear in any given situation because circumstances differ. It is difficult to find a particular pattern of conduct that will always be right, and so we are interested in this part of his Epistle to the Romans to hear what Paul has to say. We will see in verses 8-14 that Paul speaks of what I call an "omnibus principle."

By "omnibus" I mean that this principle will be like a bus that carries everyone. Here is a general principle that covers all conduct on the part of a believer: everything he does should be done for the welfare and happiness of others. And here the emphasis is on "others."

> Owe no man any thing, but to love one another: for he that loveth another hath fulfilled the law (Rom. 13:8).

Do not go into debt, and that is true not only of money; the believer is not to be under obligation to anyone. Do not impose upon people. As a believer in God, live in such a way that you pay your way as you go along. There is only one obligation you should accept: the universal obligation to help and serve. In serving others a person will fulfill the law of God because this is what God does. He makes His sun to shine on the good and the bad and His rain to fall on the just and the unjust. If we are to be the children of our Father in heaven we must have an attitude toward people to seek their welfare at all times. This is not because they deserve it but because we have the grace of God in our hearts.

> For this, Thou shalt not commit adultery, Thou shalt not kill, Thou shalt not steal, Thou shalt not bear false witness, Thou shalt not covet; and if there be any other commandment, it is briefly comprehended in this saying, namely, Thou shalt love thy neighbour as thyself (Rom. 13:9).

Here is a restatement of most of the second part of the Ten Commandments, although the precepts are not in the same order. Of course, the last part of the verse is what the Bible calls the second great commandment. This does not say "Thou shalt love thy neighbor instead of thyself," but "Thou shalt love thy neighbor *as* thyself." Here again the word *love* is not merely appreciation, feeling, or adoring; it is a matter of serving. "Love worketh no ill to his neighbour: therefore love is the fulfilling of the law" (Rom. 13:10). Doing for others is not harmful and it is therefore right.

> And that, knowing the time, that now it is high time to awake out of sleep: for now is our salvation nearer than when we believed. The night is far spent, the day is at hand: let us therefore cast off the works of darkness, and let us put on the armour of light (Rom. 13:11,12).

Time is short. Today is the day. Your lifetime is short, and it is later than you think. Do not put off until next month going to church, reading the Bible, and praying. Do it now.

> Let us walk honestly, as in the day; not in rioting and drunkenness, not in chambering and wantonness, not in strife and envying. But put ye on the Lord Jesus Christ, and make not provision for the flesh, to fulfil the lusts thereof (Rom. 13:13,14).

Do not plan for your own enjoyment and the satisfaction of the lusts of the flesh. Keep in mind that the things of the Lord are first and foremost.

Let me remind you again that this portion of Romans is written only for believers in God.

Chapter 56

RECEIVING THE WEAK

(Romans 14:1-4)

Many people do not fully understand the gospel. How can believers, who know more, help such people?

> Him that is weak in the faith receive ye, but not to doubtful disputations (Rom. 14:1).

Here Paul speaks about people who do not completely understand the gospel. Believers should welcome any person into their fellowship, even if he has a limited understanding of the gospel, but they should avoid arguing. Paul discusses this as well as other limitations in this chapter. These limitations apply to daily living, and essential to their operation in our lives is the matter of personal relationship to the Lord Jesus Christ. Paul says, "If any man love not the Lord Jesus Christ, let him be Anathema [cast away]" (1 Cor. 16:22).

This chapter deals with people who believe in the Lord Jesus Christ but who have different ideas about their conduct. The illustration in verses 2-4 concerns the proper food to be eaten. Perhaps everyone knows the Jewish custom that people must eat kosher food, and this is especially true of meat. It is not right to eat food that is not kosher. In the early Christian church the question came up, Did this Jewish regulation about food continue to have application among Christian believers? Paul found that there were some believers who said yes and others who said no.

> For one believeth that he may eat all things: another, who is weak, eateth herbs (Rom. 14:2).

This was particularly significant for some of the Gentiles because they had customs in their pagan temples of dedicating food to their pagan gods. Some of the food was offered to the various gods and was so designated.

There were sensitive believers in Christ who felt they should not eat food offered to idols, while others felt it did not make any difference because the food was just as good as it had been before. The result was that some would be so cautious they would not eat meat at all; they were vegetarians because they did not want to break any rules. Paul gave his judgment about this problem:

> Let not him that eateth despise him that eateth not; and let not him which eateth not judge him that eateth: for God hath received him (Rom. 14:3).

Paul is saying the person who feels free to eat any kind of meat should not despise the person who does not feel free to do so. If he had liberty within himself and felt free to do this, there would be a tendency to despise the man who seemed to be narrow in his views. Believers who feel broad-minded are inclined to belittle and sometimes despise others they think are narrow. "And let not him which eateth not judge him that eateth." Some who refrained from eating meat for fear it was meat offered to idols would not eat meat at all. They were critical of those who felt free to eat any meat.

Some believers are extremely careful in their own conduct, and when they see other believers allowing themselves greater freedom they condemn them. Paul speaks against this kind of criticism and tells them not to judge one another.

> Who art thou that judgest another man's servant? to his own master he standeth or falleth. Yea, he shall be holden up: for God is able to make him stand (Rom. 14:4).

Critical appraisal of our brethren is not our privilege. Only God can judge, and He is more concerned to save than He is to condemn.

There will be differences in interpretation. Christians do not always see things exactly alike, and each will apply Scripture differently to his conduct. But it is not the privilege of anyone to condemn another believer because of his conduct. Of course, God will and does judge, but Paul states here that when God judges, He is gracious. This is not to say that one man's conduct is as good as another but that the other man's conduct is not anyone else's business. Each believer's conduct is his business before God. Even though another believer should not criticize him, that does not mean that God could not criticize him. We will see in the next study that every man is going to stand before the judgment seat of Christ.

Chapter 57

INDIVIDUAL RESPONSIBILITY

(Romans 14:5-12)

Do you realize that whereas no believer needs to explain his actions to any other believer, we must all answer to Jesus Christ?

> Let every man be fully persuaded in his own mind (Rom. 14:5).

This is the way the apostle Paul states the broad principle that should govern the attitude of any believer toward the conduct of himself and others. Believers are not to judge one another, and the conduct of any believer is his own responsibility; Paul is now emphasizing that every believer is responsible only to Christ. Each of us shall give account of himself to God.

Paul uses an illustration with reference to special days — holy days, the Sabbath, Good Friday, Easter Sunday, Christmas, etc.:

> One man esteemeth one day above another: another esteemeth every day alike (Rom. 14:5).

One believer will make a distinction between the days, while another will treat them all the same. Often people will ask me about this, and frankly I feel that every day I live is a Sabbath day. And I do make some difference in my conduct on Sunday. Yet not everyone feels this way, and Paul asserts that every person should be fully persuaded in his own mind.

> He that regardeth the day, regardeth it unto the Lord; and he that regardeth not the day, to the Lord he doth not regard it (Rom. 14:6a).

Some people think the Sabbath is to be a day of rest. When they engage in certain activities, they feel this is resting and acceptable. Another person will feel they are wrong. Each believer should act as unto the Lord, according to Paul.

> He that eateth, eateth to the Lord, for he giveth God thanks; and he that eateth not, to the Lord he eateth not, and giveth God thanks. For none of us liveth to himself, and no man dieth to himself (Rom. 14:6,7).

A believer does not live by himself; he lives in the sight of God.

> For whether we live, we live unto the Lord; and whether we die, we die unto the Lord: whether we live therefore, or die, we are the Lord's. For to this end Christ both died, and rose, and revived, that he might be Lord both of the dead and living. But why dost thou judge thy brother? or why dost thou set at nought thy brother? for we shall all stand before the judgment seat of Christ (Rom. 14:8-10).

Paul has been describing many differences of opinion toward proper conduct. Our opinions may differ, but there should be no difference in our attitude toward the Lord and our responsibility to Him. However, if we believe in Christ our attitude toward others, especially toward other believers, should not be judgmental, for Christ alone will judge.

> For it is written, As I live, saith the Lord, every knee shall bow to me, and every tongue shall confess to God. So then every one of us shall give account of himself to God (Rom. 14:11,12).

This is basic. Paul wants each believer to have an openhearted attitude toward other believers. We can be united and walk together because each of us is responsible to the Lord who is watching over us.

Chapter 58

ATTITUDE TOWARD BRETHREN

(Romans 14:13-15)

Since each believer is responsible only to God for his conduct, should any believer think of others as he lives from day to day?

> Let us not therefore judge one another any more: but judge this rather, that no man put a stumblingblock or an occasion to fall in his brother's way (Rom. 14:13).

Thus far we have seen two major points in this chapter. First, we should not judge each other; second, even though we do not judge each other, we should remember we are responsible to God. Now we are to see something further: we should judge ourselves. Each person should criticize himself in terms of the effect his conduct has upon others.

Wherever we see the word *judge* we can substitute the word *criticize*, because the Greek word for judge is *kritikos*, from which we get the word *critic*. How do our actions affect others? If our conduct causes another person to stumble — if it offends or raises questions in his mind and makes him doubt us, himself, and God — then we are a stumbling block. If we cause another who may be following us to fall into vice, we are a stumbling block. So I raise these questions about our conduct: How does it affect other people? Is it dangerous? Is it questionable? As believers we must accept responsibility for the effect of our example on other believers who may not be as strong as we are.

In this passage of Scripture is found one of the most amazing statements in the New Testament:

> I know, and am persuaded by the Lord Jesus, that there is nothing unclean of itself (Rom. 14:14a).

Sometimes I consider that statement in this way: there is nothing a human being can do which, in itself, is necessarily evil.

> But to him that esteemeth any thing to be unclean, to him it is unclean (Rom. 14:14b).

By way of illustration, opium is a drug few people use. It can be used as a medicine in a doctor's prescription, but used the wrong way it causes deterioration of an individual's personality. We would consider that to be unclean. Alcohol, in the way it is commonly used, has become unclean also.

> But if thy brother be grieved with thy meat, now walkest thou not charitably (Rom. 14:15a).

If you allow yourself to do anything you please because you feel free to do it, and your conduct grieves your brother, actually affecting him for evil, it is not right. His welfare is involved.

Then comes this strong word:

> Destroy not him with thy meat, for whom Christ died (Rom. 14:15b).

If there is a person who believes in Jesus Christ and, for some reason of his own, eats and drinks and does what he pleases, and by so doing sets an example which results in harm to the other person, he is doing wrong. Christ died for that weaker brother. If Christ died for him, should we not be careful that what we do does not hurt him?

Chapter 59

SEEKING PEACE

(Romans 14:16-19)

Do you know what should be the most important ambition in the life of a child of God?

> Let us therefore follow after the things which make for peace (Rom. 14:19a).

These are the words with which Paul summarizes his discussion of our interest in other people and our personal conduct.

> Let not then your good be evil spoken of (Rom. 14:16).

What Paul is saying is this: what you have found to be good in the gospel and in the freedom that is in the Lord Jesus Christ is that it does not depend upon you to win your salvation. Salvation is given to you through Christ Jesus, who will save you because of His grace and mercy. You do not buy it nor work for it: it is a free gift from God. However, Paul emphasizes the fact that believers should not act carelessly on that account.

> For the kingdom of God is not meat and drink; but righteousness, and peace, and joy in the Holy Ghost (Rom. 14:17).

The "kingdom of God" refers to the relationship believers have with God in Christ, where God is the ruler of their lives and they are obedient to Him. We know that meat and drink have to do with our conduct in this world, but the kingdom of God involves more than that. The spiritual values of the gospel are what really matter: being right in God's sight. And the results of that are peace, being right in relation to others, and joy, being right with reference to the Lord Jesus Christ and our own souls. It does not mean that food and activity of any sort do not matter, but they are not as important as our relationship with God.

> For he that in these things serveth Christ is acceptable to God, and approved of men (Rom. 14:18).

This may be applied to conduct as well as to the qualities righteousness, peace, and joy. Some may wonder why a child of God should care about other people. As members of Christ's body they want to win souls because Christ died for them. God wants all men to know about Him, and His children are His witnesses, the light shining in darkness.

> Let your light so shine before men, that they may see your good works, and glorify your Father which is in heaven (Matt. 5:16).
>
> Let us therefore follow after the things which make for peace, and things wherewith one may edify another (Rom. 14:19).

To *follow after* means to "pursue." Let us pursue those things that make for peace with God. Let us confess our sins and draw near and worship Him. Let us follow after the things which make for peace with other believers by being careful in our conduct and not judging them, but conducting ourselves honestly and openly in the presence of others. Our conduct can have the effect upon others of building them up in the things that have to do with faith, understanding, and knowledge. Let us walk so that people following us will believe that Christ is real, that the gospel is real, and that God is real. In that way we can nurture faith in Him. This should be the general purpose of our lives, and God will bless us.

Chapter 60

RESPONSIBLE FAITH

(Romans 14:20-23)

Do you realize that a child of God should not only try to do what is right, but also try to do what looks right to others?

> For meat destroy not the work of God (Rom. 14:20a).

Paul exhorts believers to not let their conduct, their habits and personal pleasures, harm other people. He continues to talk about the attitude and the conduct of believers toward others, admonishing that nothing be done to upset another spiritually. The personal conduct of an evangelical believer could injure and confuse others, even other believers. Paul now makes an important statement:

> All things indeed are pure; but it is evil for that man who eateth with offence (Rom. 14:20b).

It is possible to do something which in itself may be innocent, but the way in which it is done can cause harm to others and affect the one doing it. It is not enough to say there is nothing wrong with what one does. The question is, Does it appear wrong to others?

> It is good neither to eat flesh, nor to drink wine, nor any thing whereby thy brother stumbleth, or is offended, or is made weak (Rom. 14:21).

This is the general negative truth about liberty in conduct. Believers are free to do as they want to do in the sight of God; but they should act with care because their personal conduct matters to others. They should take into account that if they act to lead a person into trouble, then they are going in the wrong direction.

> Hast thou faith? have it to thyself before God (Rom. 14:22a).

If the believer's conscience is clear, he should thank the Lord; but he must continue to be careful how he acts in the presence of other people. "Happy is he that condemneth not himself in that thing which he alloweth" (Rom. 14:22b).

> And he that doubteth is damned if he eat, because he eateth not of faith: for whatsoever is not of faith is sin (Rom. 14:23).

This, in my estimation, is the strongest definition of sin in the Bible. The person who is not sure about the full meaning of his conduct, yet goes ahead and does it anyway, is condemned because he did not act in faith. He was not clear in his own mind that he had clearance from the Lord, so he was aware it might even be wrong. The very fact that he thought it might be wrong and yet did it means he was willing to do it even if it was wrong, and that is sin. If he eats when he doubts whether he should — for example, if he eats meat offered to idols when he feels in his heart it may not be right — that is wrong. When he did it he was not satisfied it was pleasing to God, thus he was not acting in faith.

This brings to mind several definitions of sin. The first and simplest definition is any act contrary to God's will. When God said to Adam, "Ye shall not eat of it," Adam sinned the moment he ate. Here we see sin as an act of disobedience to God's expressed will. Jesus said that if a man looks upon a woman in a certain way he has already committed adultery with her in his heart. The very intention is counted as evil. Anything that hinders or hurts other people is sin. If anything I do causes my brother to stumble, I sin against Christ when I wound the brother's weak conscience.

There is another familiar passage in Scripture, "Therefore to him that knoweth to do good, and doeth it not, to him it is sin" (James 4:17). But here in Romans we have the highest level of the definition of sin: "Whatsoever is not of faith is sin" (Rom. 14:23). Every action I take is in the presence of God. Anything that is carried out when I am not conscious of the reality of God is sin. If I do not have approval from the Lord for my conduct, it is wrong.

Chapter 61

PLEASING OTHERS

(Romans 15:1-3)

Did you know that the first concern a believer should have about his conduct is its effect upon others?

> We then that are strong ought to bear the infirmities of the weak, and not to please ourselves (Rom. 15:1).

This is clear-cut guidance. Paul uses these two words — *strong* and *weak* — to refer to degrees of understanding. He realized that some understand the gospel better than others; these are stronger. This does not have to do directly with their personal faith in Christ; this faith could be either strong or weak. Paul has been discussing wisdom in conduct and the attitudes of mind and heart. Some people seem to be able to grasp clearly the whole meaning of the gospel at one time and then act accordingly. These are the strong. Others, though they recognize the gospel, are not able to keep it in mind at all times; and when they start deciding how to act they can become narrow. They are weak because they do not understand all that God is doing for them. Many of these people are actually superior in their standards and values. Believers should notice that they are to bear the infirmities of the weak, not to bear with the weak, but to carry them through, and not to please themselves. Believers are not in any given situation free to see what they can get out of it for themselves.

There may be a man who claims to be honest, but who feels he should not be required to keep records or report on what he does to anyone else. If he is honest, why would he object to making records, or object to telling people what he has done? He is strong, but others may be weak. If the weak brother wants him to keep a record to show what he has done he should do so. Those who are strong should bear the infirmities of the weak and not to please themselves.

> Let every one of us please his neighbour for his good to edification (Rom. 15:2).

I do not think this standard applies to everyone in the community. Let every believer please his neighbor "for his good to edification." This does not mean to please the neighbor in every way the neighbor wants him to, but in the ways that will help the neighbor grow in the things of the Lord.

> For even Christ pleased not himself; but, as it is written, The reproaches of them that reproached thee fell on me (Rom. 15:3).

This will involve sympathetic wear and tear for every believer. If you are a believer with an open heart before God and you really want to help people, you will find that many times you will become discouraged because people seem to be so weak. But you will be made patient and strong if you are in the Lord, because He never crushed the smoking flax, He never threw away the broken reed. Our Lord will be gracious and merciful to each person. Some are hard for you to tolerate, but you will live as quietly, humbly, and sincerely with these people as possible, because you want to glorify the name of the Lord Jesus Christ.

Chapter 62

GLORIFYING GOD

(Romans 15:4-13)

Do you know that people with different backgrounds can live together in harmony and glorify God?

> That ye may with one mind and one mouth glorify God, even the Father of our Lord Jesus Christ (Rom. 15:6).

The glory of God is seen in the realization of His purpose. When His will is fulfilled in any given situation, and when people who are in the Lord Jesus Christ speak with one mind and one heart, then God is being glorified. Wherever you have three men you usually have three points of view. Some may try to get the three men to think and act like one, but words alone will not accomplish this. The men must be knit together with one mind, one heart, and one mouth. Paul says that this can be done by having Christ in the heart. He also speaks of the part the Bible plays in bringing this to pass:

> For whatsoever things were written aforetime were written for our learning, that we through patience and comfort of the scriptures might have hope (Rom. 15:4).

The Scriptures, then, were written that we might have hope about everything that is in the will of God.

> Now the God of patience and consolation grant you to be likeminded one toward another according to Christ Jesus: that ye may with one mind and one mouth glorify God, even the Father of our Lord Jesus Christ (Rom. 15:5,6).

The way believers can have one mind is for them to have the mind of Christ, which they receive from the Bible. The more believers understand the Bible the closer they will be to each other. Some believe it is impossible for people to live together in unity; but they do not know about Bible study. There is one

Lord; and when people come together in Him, God has accomplished His purpose. This is to His glory.

The only way the Jew and the Gentile can come together is for the Jew to receive the Gentile and for the Gentile to receive the Jew.

> Wherefore receive ye one another, as Christ also received us to the glory of God (Rom. 15:7).

The only way for people who are trained in the Bible to get along with people who are not so trained is for the people who are trained in the Bible to patiently receive those who are not. All persons can meet as one in the Lord. This is done not for human reasons but for spiritual reasons, to the glory of God.

> Now I say that Jesus Christ was a minister of the circumcision for the truth of God, to confirm the promises made unto the fathers (Rom. 15:8).

This is another way of saying that salvation came first to the Jews, and then to the Gentiles. Christ Jesus was born of the tribe of Judah in the house of David, so He had this social heritage. He was a Jew, yet He spoke so that all Gentiles could come together in Him; not because He became a Gentile, nor that they became Jews, but because they yielded to Him, and He received them. Jesus Christ was a minister of the circumcision; He was a minister of the Jews for the truth of God to confirm the promises made to their fathers. Now Paul lists some of the promises:

> And that the Gentiles might glorify God for his mercy; as it is written, For this cause I will confess to thee among the Gentiles, and sing unto thy name (Rom. 15:9).

Eternally it had been God's plan that the Messiah would come to lead His people into salvation. Christ would speak in such a way that the Gentiles could and would come, and this is what Jesus actually did. In the early church the Jew and the Gentile lived together in quietness and peace since God had accomplished His purpose. He had overcome the wall of difference between them because they were one in the Lord.

> And again he saith, Rejoice, ye Gentiles, with his people (Rom. 15:10).

His people were the Jews but the Gentiles are to rejoice with them, not because everyone is a Gentile, and not because everyone is a Jew, and not because Gentiles and Jews no longer differ from each other, but because both are believers. That is the secret of this problem of unity.

> And again, Praise the Lord, all ye Gentiles; and laud him, all ye people. And again, [Isaiah] saith, There shall be a root of Jesse, and he that shall rise to reign over the Gentiles; in him shall the Gentiles trust (Rom. 15:11,12).

These are the promises of the Old Testament, and here Paul is simply claiming that the Lord Jesus Christ has completed His work in such a way that He is the fulfillment of the Old Testament promises.

> Now the God of hope fill you with all joy and peace in believing, that ye may abound in hope, through the power of the Holy Ghost (Rom. 15:13).

Emphasis here is upon the word *hope,* confident expectation of the future. It is in the confident expectation of the future that the Jew and the Gentile will join together, because they know the day has come when one is not a Jew and the other is not a Gentile. They can live together in peace and be filled with all joy in believing through the power of the Holy Spirit. Inasmuch as there are no divisions in heaven, neither are they felt here. So the Jew and the Gentile can be together in the Lord now, because each has the mind of the Lord, and the mind of the Lord is operative within to bring him into unity with the other members of the body of Christ.

Chapter 63

MINISTRY TO THE GENTILES

(Romans 15:14-24)

Do you realize that some believers are given responsibility to define what should be in the gospel?

In these studies in the Book of Romans we learn that Paul sets forth the meaning of the gospel with heart-searching clarity. When reading what he has written we feel we are standing in the very presence of the truth of God. Paul is writing to people who do not know him personally, having never had dealings with him. They had no way of knowing the kindness of his spirit, the warmth of his heart, or the keenness of his intellect. It is possible that some resented his direct style, for he minced no words. He openly pointed out that "all have sinned, and come short of the glory of God."

When we look at Romans 15:14-24 we see how Paul points out the ground of his confidence. He assures these Christians that he has a good opinion of them.

> And I myself also am persuaded of you, my brethren, that ye also are full of goodness, filled with all knowledge, able also to admonish one another (Rom. 15:14).

He assures them that he believes they have virtue and understanding and are capable of judging themselves.

> Nevertheless, brethren, I have written the more boldly unto you in some sort, as putting you in mind, because of the grace that is given to me of God, that I should be the minister of Jesus Christ to the Gentiles, ministering the gospel of God, that the offering up of the Gentiles might be acceptable, being sanctified by the Holy Ghost (Rom. 15:15,16).

The use of the word *brethren* seems to indicate that Paul wants to be close to them. Paul was given the responsibility of being the authorized spokesman, the one who represented the gospel to the Gentiles so that in coming before God they might be acceptable to him. One who preaches the gospel sets forth the truth clearly so the people who believe are able to keep the record accurate. Paul has written plainly that people should bring nothing of the flesh — they should put this away. These people would be acceptable not because of work they had done, but because of what they understood, and because of their willingness to yield themselves to the Lord.

Apparently Paul had been especially endowed with power to work wonders by the Holy Spirit. He not only talked but worked.

> I have therefore whereof I may glory through Jesus Christ in those things which pertain to God. For I will not dare to speak of any of those things which Christ hath not wrought by me, to make the Gentiles obedient, by word and deed, through mighty signs and wonders, by the power of the Spirit of God; so that from Jerusalem, and round about unto Illyricum, I have fully preached the gospel of Christ (Rom. 15:17-19).

Paul had preached the gospel of Christ with amazing results, and God had given him this power. Some of the results may have been physical miracles, but many were spiritual miracles, in which lives were changed. Some of the results were such that by the power of his preaching, faith was engendered in people. This gave Paul strength when he taught.

He had followed the policy of going only into such sections of the country where the gospel was not preached.

> Yea, so have I strived to preach the gospel, not where Christ was named, lest I should build upon another man's foundation: but as it is written, To whom he was not spoken of, they shall see: and they that have not heard shall understand (Rom. 15:20,21).

Because he was doing this he was delayed in getting over to Rome — "For which cause also I have been much hindered from coming to you" (Rom. 15:22).

Now he felt that he had finished his work and was free to travel again. He planned to go into Spain on the other side of Italy after first preaching among the believers in Rome (Rom. 15:23,24). Paul felt free to plan this program because of the blessings he had received. God had so blessed his ministry that Paul knew he was in the will of God. The people also knew he was in the will of God because they saw the results. This gave Paul additional freedom to speak to them.

Chapter 64

MINISTRY TO THE BELIEVERS

(Romans 15:25-33)

Can you believe that a preacher might have more trouble dealing with church people than he would have in dealing with the world?

In the Book of Romans we have the opportunity to look into the affairs of a real man of God. Paul was an outstanding person, and when we read what he said and did, we can learn much about what it means to be a real believer. Paul asked the people in Rome to pray for him that he might be blessed when he went to the mother church in Jerusalem. The younger churches in Macedonia had heard that the older churches in Jerusalem were in need, so they took up an offering and sent it to Jerusalem with Paul. Paul was aware that these people were believers before he was converted and I suspect he felt a certain uneasiness about going among them. Paul felt that such consideration of their plight was proper; after all, the older believers had sent the gospel to the younger ones. It seemed only right that the younger believers now should send money to the older group. The apostle planned his program with regard to what was practical.

> When therefore I have performed this, and have sealed to them this fruit, I will come by you into Spain. And I am sure that, when I come unto you, I shall come in the fullness of the blessing of the gospel of Christ (Rom. 15:28,29).

Jerusalem is on the eastern side of the Mediterranean Sea and Spain is on the western side; Rome lies between the two. This is a simple way of pointing out the practical nature of Paul's plan. He expected his ministry among them to be fruitful in spiritual blessing; his visit would not be a social one. Paul asks for four different things: first, he calls for prayer support in his program, reasoning that spiritually it was important that those in Jerusalem would accept the gift, and especially important that, when he moved on, he would be blessed of God.

> Now I beseech you, brethren, for the Lord Jesus Christ's sake, and for the love of the Spirit, that ye strive together with me in your prayers to God for me (Rom. 15:30).

Secondly Paul asked that he might be delivered to be free to preach:

> That I may be delivered from them that do not believe in Judea (Rom. 15:31a).

These people who did not believe and who hindered Paul were not renegade Jews. They may even have been members of the church. But they were people who were not actively exercising faith in Jesus Christ. There can be church members who look on other people on a human, rather than spiritual level. Paul indicated he wanted to be delivered from those who did not believe, both within and outside the church. He feared that they would, in their human way as Jews in Jerusalem, be critical of him and resist him because he ministered among the Gentiles.

> And that my service which I have for Jerusalem may be accepted of the saints (Rom. 15:31b).

Paul did not want to turn the money over to them and not be appreciated. Such esteem on the part of the people of Jerusalem would be the blessing of God. Paul prayed that the hearts of the believers in Jerusalem would be open; he wanted them to appreciate this gift from the people in Macedonia.

> That I may come unto you with joy by the will of God, and may with you be refreshed (Rom. 15:32).

Paul wanted his visit to be a spiritual encouragement to the people in Rome and to himself. For that he would need the blessing of God, and for this he prayed.

> Now the God of peace be with you all. Amen (Rom. 15:33).

Here Paul sums up the first fifteen chapters of the Book of Romans. He began by showing them how they needed salvation, how God had provided this salvation freely in Christ, how it would be effectual in them by the Holy Spirit, and how, by the grace of God working in their hearts, there would be results in their lives glorifying to God and a great help to them.

We can have the hope and the prayer if we have come to this place in the Book of Romans that our hearts, also, will be blessed through the truth we have found.

Chapter 65

SALUTATIONS

(Romans 16:1-7)

Do you realize that children of God can and do serve the Lord by their good reputation in the community?

When we came to the end of chapter 15 we saw the little word *amen*, and in a sense this marks the end of the treatment of the general topic of salvation as it has been set forth in Romans. In chapter 16 we will note Paul's reference to certain other persons. We begin to form an idea of the community of believers. To a certain degree the life of faith is centered in the heart, affected by those with whom we associate.

The opening verses concern a woman named Phoebe. She is of special interest because apparently she was a leader in the church. Because she was a woman, this raises a question with many people.

> I commend unto you [Phoebe] our sister, which is a servant of the church which is at Cenchrea (Rom. 16:1).

The English word *servant* does not seem significant, but in the Greek the word is *deacon*. Actually it is the word for *deaconess*. We do not know exactly what procedure the early church followed when it elected elders and deacons. It is possible there was not a precise job description for such leaders, though it is undoubtedly true they did function in some way in the service of the church. Phoebe was moving to Rome, and Paul writes ahead so they will receive her as a believer and as a trusted fellow worker.

> That ye receive her in the Lord, as becometh saints, and that ye assist her in whatsoever business she hath need of you: for she hath been a succourer of many, and of myself also (Rom. 16:2).

Paul wanted this woman to have a fraternal welcome in

Rome and that she be assisted in any project of service. It is not clearly indicated what kind of service she would render, but we have an idea there would be things that needed to be done that an understanding and intelligent believing woman could do.

> Greet Priscilla and Aquila my helpers in Christ Jesus (Rom. 16:3).

It is recorded that when Paul went to Corinth he lived in the home of Priscilla and Aquila — Aquila being a Jew who was exiled from Rome by the edict of the emperor Claudius. Both Paul and Aquila were tentmakers. We are told in Acts 18 that Aquila and Priscilla did something very significant. When they heard the eloquent and zealous young Apollos preach the gospel and realized that he understood the ways of God only through the baptism of John and thus did not have the whole truth of the gospel: ". . . they took him unto them, and expounded unto him the way of God more perfectly" (Acts 18:26). Their grasp of the truth was profound, and that Apollos would listen to them and learn from them speaks well for him.

Paul says further about Priscilla and Aquila:

> Who have for my life laid down their own necks (Rom. 16:4).

They risked their own lives to help Paul. We can learn something important from them. "Likewise greet the church that is in their house" (Rom. 16:5a). This is one use of the word *church* where it refers to the local group. The word *church* is used several different ways in the New Testament. In a deep sense we call the church the "body of Christ." We think of ourselves as members of His body. Also, the church is spoken of as the "bride of Christ." In all these different words, believers living in this world and those who have already gone to glory, as well as those who will be born, are all taken together in the "church."

When we speak of the "church triumphant" we are thinking of the members who have gone on to heaven. Such use of the word *church* refers to the "one church." We use the word *church* to refer to any group of believers as, for instance, in verse 4, "but also all the churches of the Gentiles." Here it refers to local congregations and even denominations in the plural. When we refer to "the church that is in their house" we are referring to a local group of believers. They did not have a church building; they met in the home of Priscilla and Aquila. They were similar to what we would call a prayer meeting group.

Now note carefully as we read:

> Salute my well-beloved Epenetus, who is the firstfruits of Achaia unto Christ. Greet Mary, who bestowed much labour on us. Salute Andronicus and Junia, my kinsmen, and my fellow prisoners, who are of note among the apostles, who also were in Christ before me (Rom. 16:5b-7).

These believers had prestige in the church in Jerusalem. They were committed to Christ before Paul was. This passage shows that Paul was extremely conscious of those around him who are in the Lord's service.

Chapter 66

MORE SALUTATIONS

(Romans 16:8-16)

Can you understand how fellowship among believers would be promoted by recognizing individuals in the group who are known by their works?

It is important for a believer to have fellowship with other believers, not only in church life but also in his private life. Such fellowship is promoted when believers recognize and appreciate what others have done, and especially when they esteem those who are of good report. It is sad that in some of our congregations that the common report in the group and about the group is of the evil that has occurred. This should not be. The truth is that you will know a church better when you know its strength and when you know the good people in it.

How do we really know men or women? By their faults or by their virtues? Jesus of Nazareth taught, "By their fruits ye shall know them" (Matt. 7:20). Paul is sending salutations to these people in Rome about certain persons, and in verses 8-16 we do not find one fault pointed out. No doubt these people had faults, and Paul may have known about them, but nothing was said about them.

Something is said about every person for us to remember and to appreciate about them.

> Greet Amplias my beloved in the Lord (Rom. 16:8).

That is all; that was the kind of man he was.

> Salute Urbane, our helper in Christ, and Stachys my beloved (Rom. 16:9).

Urbane helped. Did he make mistakes? Probably. Was he perfect? No. Paul called this man, Stachys, "my beloved."

> Salute Apelles approved in Christ (Rom. 16:10a).

How much money did he make last year? That is not the point. Nor did it matter what kind of clothes he wore. It is only important that he was "approved in Christ."

> Salute them which are of Aristobulus' household. Salute Herodion my kinsman. Greet them that be of the household of Narcissus, which are in the Lord (Rom. 16:10b,11).

Here evidently were men of note and members of their families were to be shown consideration.

> Salute [Tryphaena] and Tryphosa, who labour in the Lord. Salute the beloved Persis, which laboured much in the Lord (Rom. 16:12).

These beloved persons worked hard for the Lord.

> Salute Rufus chosen in the Lord, and his mother and mine (Rom. 16:13).

That is all that is said about him, but it is enough.

In verse 14 there is a list of names that ends with these words:

> Salute Asyncritus, Phlegon, Hermas, Patrobas, Hermes, and the brethren which are with them (Rom. 16:14).

Anyone with that group was to be treated well. Paul is not guiding them to pass judgment on these persons: he is asking them to receive these believers. God will pass judgment.

> Salute Philologus, and Julia, Nereus, and his sister, and Olympas, and all the saints which are with them (Rom. 16:15).

All the people who associate with these folks are to be treated cordially.

> Salute one another with a holy kiss (Rom. 16:16a).

Greet one another with Christian affection. You may not have reason to appreciate those people on a human level, but you are dealing with them as believers. Salute them.

> The churches of Christ salute you (Rom. 16:16b).

All of the believers Paul knew were sending their greetings. This is a wonderful guidance for our attitude toward other believing people. May the Lord bless every one of them.

Chapter 67

AVOID DIVISIONS

(Romans 16:17-20)

Are you aware of teachers who cause division and offense among believers?

From the beginning of creation God has permitted Satan to tempt people to turn away from His will. Usually the temptation comes in the guise of something "better" than they already have. The real significance of the temptation is generally hidden, and the subtle character of such a tempting proposal makes caution extremely important. The situation as it develops is deceptive, and even a sincere person could be fooled. Many times when the believer has in mind what he thinks "ought" to be, there comes a suggestion of a short-cut way to secure this by his own efforts: some way to achieve this desirable result without any possible danger of loss, but leaving God out of the picture. This is dangerous.

Again and again God's people are warned in the Bible to beware of being fooled in this fashion. Our Lord warned His disciples against wolves in sheep's clothing. Keep this in mind: no one will be misled by someone who looks bad; what a person can be taken in by, what is really dangerous, is something that looks good. Usually when a person is in a situation where there is strain or stress, and usually when he is face to face with a question of what to do and how to do it, a suggestion comes that there is a better or smoother way of doing it.

Moses warned against prophets who came among the people and performed miracles impressively, but when one watched to see which way they were leading, it could be seen they were not leading toward God. Moses said not to follow those. Joshua warned his people against following after pagan gods. He challenged them, "You can go the way you want to go, but as for me and my house, we will serve the Lord." The prophets in the time of the kings in Israel warned Israel over and over against the false prophets who harassed them.

The will of God is revealed to us in the Word of God; but when the Word of God is brought to us, sometimes other words are brought also, and we are in a position where we scarcely know how to discern between them. At one time our Lord said plainly, "Take heed that no man deceive you" (Matt. 24:4). Paul warned about this in Romans 16:17:

> Now I beseech you, brethren, mark them which cause divisions and offenses contrary to the doctrine which ye have learned; and avoid them.

Such troublemakers do not say they are going to mislead; but they cause divisions and offenses because they teach a doctrine contrary to the doctrine that has been learned. For instance, Paul taught, "All have sinned, and come short of the glory of God" (Rom. 3:23). Paul goes on to say that all need to be saved. This is the truth, and when any teaching does not follow that, a division will come.

When these divisions occur, certain things should be kept in mind. Often a division will come when only a few people see the direction it is taking. They see what is wrong and may try to prevent it. But at times they are looked upon as the very persons who are causing the trouble. When the twelve spies went into the land of Canaan and returned, ten said it was impossible to go into Canaan, whereas two of them said it could be done. Can you see why Joshua and Caleb would be called troublemakers? When Moses was dealing with Pharaoh, who was willing to make concessions while Moses was not, would not Moses have been considered the one who was really causing the trouble? But he was not. People who cause divisions are those who lead away from the truth.

Many other doctrines could be mentioned. For example, men are justified by faith in Jesus Christ and not by their own works; and to be saved, one must be born again. Teaching not in line with these doctrines causes division. Paul taught that emphasis on personal righteousness is an error; he pointed out that the Jews made a mistake in that they tried to justify themselves by their own righteousness. Again, Paul said the kingdom of God is not of this world, but there are people who think differently and will say so.

What about those people? What should you do? You should avoid them. Shall we condemn them? No —avoid them. Correct them? No — avoid them. Compromise with them? No — avoid them. In verse 18 we see that they are far too subtle for us to successfully refute them. We are just not able to overcome them. Paul urges that we should be wise concerning what is good but simple toward what is evil. So, do not try to be too clever. Just walk with the Lord. This is what comes to our minds here in this part of the Book of Romans. May the Lord help us to stay close to Him.

Chapter 68

GLORY BELONGS TO GOD

(Romans 16:21-27)

Is it clear to you that there is no other name given under heaven among men whereby we must be saved?

> By me if any man enter in, he shall be saved (John 10:9).

Jesus left no room for doubt as to how you and I may be saved.

> I am the way, the truth, and the life: no man cometh unto the Father, but by me (John 14:6).

Believers have the blessing of God not by nature, man, or works, but by the call of God in Christ by the Holy Spirit, who functions in believers and who shows them the things of Christ. An important element is our faith in Jesus Himself, right now in the presence of God. The temptation that confronts all people who think at all about being saved is having seen the desirable result and then trying to achieve it by personal effort.

Abraham was the father of all believers. He considered not his own body but was strong in faith, giving glory to God, believing that what God promised He was able also to perform. This is the classic pattern. It should be mentioned again that Paul kindly but clearly stated that the Jews were the outstanding victims of this error, seeking to get right with God on the basis of their own efforts. In our last study we took note of the fact that there are active among Christian people teachers who cause divisions and offenses by teaching things that are contrary to the doctrine which they learned. But now we are to be given comforting reassurance.

> And the God of peace shall bruise Satan under your feet shortly (Rom. 16:20a).

The language here refers to Genesis 3:15, when God promised that the seed of the woman would bruise the head of the serpent. Jesus of Nazareth was none other than the seed of the woman, and here the promise is repeated that He should bruise Satan under His feet. This is the promise that in due time Christ will completely crush this untrue procedure that had been suggested to them. Then Paul prays:

> The grace of our Lord Jesus Christ be with you. Amen (Rom. 16:20b).

It will not be their strength, but His.

In verses 21-23 Paul calls upon his fellow workers, all of whom agreed with this message to the people in Rome. There is a wonderful benediction in verses 25-27 in which Paul reiterates that all glory for such a salvation belongs to God.

> Now to him that is of power to stablish you according to my gospel, and the preaching of Jesus Christ (Rom. 16:25a).

Paul started out wanting to give them the spiritual truth that would establish them.

The preaching of Jesus Christ is much more than repeating His name. It is taking the things of Jesus Christ and His eternal life, and not only referring to them but showing what they can mean. For instance, consider His crucifixion: here the flesh is put to death and the only way out of sin is to die in the flesh as Christ died on Calvary so that we are crucified with Him. We reckon we are buried with Him. Then we are risen from the dead with Him in the power of God. Paul preached Jesus Christ, implying to those who heard, "You can be raised from the dead that you might now, as children of God, receive the Holy Spirit of God; He will never leave you nor forsake you as long as you continue to live. For eternity there will be an unending, unbroken communion with God. You are to come into fellowship with God and this is what will establish you."

> According to the revelation of the mystery, which was kept secret since the world began, but now is made manifest, and by the scriptures of the prophets, according to the commandment of the everlasting God, made known to all nations for the obedience of faith (Rom. 16:25b,26).

This mystery which has been hidden is now made manifest. It

can be spread by the Scriptures of the prophets.

That cannot be overstated. The only way people will ever come to know God in Christ Jesus is through the Scriptures, where they learn the Bible message. As they come to know these things they can enter into them. Paul concludes this whole epistle thus:

> To God only wise, be glory through Jesus Christ for ever. Amen (Rom. 16:27).

I hope and trust this will include you. Christ Jesus came for you. You can be saved in Him. He asks you to come to Him.

Chapter 69

THE MYSTERY OF GOD

(Romans 16:25-27)

Are you ready to accept the idea that something was revealed through Jesus Christ that was never before known, and you cannot know it now except in the gospel?

God is. This is known throughout the world. The Scriptures tell us "the fool hath said in his heart there is no God" and "the heavens declare the glory of God, the firmament showeth his handiwork." Even the devils believe there is one God, although they believe it in fear and trembling. This is not new, and this is not the "mystery of God."

God is judge. This is not new. Everyone who has any sense of responsibility believes that his Creator is his Judge.

God is good. We do not have to read that in a book. Paul reminded the heathen people at Lystra that this was common knowledge. We are reminded by fruitful seasons and by all the blessings of nature that God is good.

God is gracious. In Romans, Paul tells us that the kindness and goodness of God lead us to repentance.

God is holy and righteous. This is no surprise. The Ten Commandments are self-evident, and when we read them we know they are valid. There may be one or two commandments we do not understand because of the circumstances in which they were written, but everyone understands, for example, "Thou shalt not steal."

God is merciful. Many people trust the mercy of God.

Not one of the above ideas is new although not everyone accepts them. Those who read books on philosophy about the writings of the ancients — even the Greeks like Plato and Aristotle — say it is remarkable how much they said about God that was true. In the writings of the Romans there were pagan men who wrote about God. There were things the Chinese knew through Confucius about God the Creator that are true. Yet there is something new in the gospel. It was a mystery that was kept secret since the world began.

In our day the various processes of electricity are common knowledge to us. A few hundred years ago no one ever dreamed of electricity. As intelligent as the ancient Greeks were, they had no conception of it. But do you realize there was electricity in the world all the time? It was a hidden truth. It existed but no one saw it. In our generation oil was discovered in east Texas. Men had abandoned their farms because they were unable to make a living on that land. Unfortunately they did not know there was a hidden fortune under it. It was a "mystery" in the sense Paul uses the word in the New Testament.

Now we raise the question: Can we find out what this "mystery" was? What was it that was true all the time but was never seen until the coming of the Lord Jesus Christ? Very simply, this was the great truth: This creation — this world we live in — was started and it will stop. This temporary mortal life, with birth and death, is vulnerable to sin, but this was not God's final plan for us. This was not the end toward which God began His creation process. The marvelous truth that was revealed in Christ Jesus is that Adam, the first man, was not the final work of God. The final work of God is not creation but salvation. Jesus was the Lamb slain before the foundation of the world. Before God made this world He knew men would fail and Christ would come and save those who would put their trust in Him. God's purpose would not be fulfilled in Adam but in His Son, Jesus the Christ.

This was true from the beginning, and it was no surprise to God when Adam failed. This was a first draft of the plan, but He had a permanent one coming up. The Son of man would do God's will perfectly and would live forever. Then it would be revealed that "whosoever believeth in him would not perish but have everlasting life." Whoever believed in Jesus Christ and invited Him to live in him would fulfill the righteousness of God. This is the great truth that is to be seen in Christ Jesus, what the people in the Old Testament never knew, and yet they looked forward to it. Moses said, "After me there will arise a prophet like unto me. Listen to him. He will tell you."

David was told that a Son of his would sit on the throne forever. His throne would be over all the other thrones. All the kingdoms of the earth would become the kingdoms of his Lord, his Christ, his Messiah, his Anointed One. Then Paul says in the concluding verses of Romans:

> . . . the mystery, which was kept secret since the world began, but now is made manifest, and by the scriptures of the prophets, according to the commandment of the everlasting God, made known to all nations for the obedience of faith (Rom. 16:25,26).

The Scriptures of the prophets include a word in Isaiah when God said He would create a new threshing instrument and with it He would do differently. In Jeremiah a New Covenant is promised. The Old Covenant told man what to do, but man could not do it. God sent His own Son into the world to do it perfectly; in Him man can make it, never in his own strength. In Christ Jesus man can obey God.

This is the mystery, the hidden truth, which was true all along but was not revealed until the coming of the Lord Jesus Christ: that believers would be saved in Him, and God would create a new heaven and a new earth in which dwelleth righteousness.